Guide to English Heritage Properties

open to the public 1990/91

English ☷ Heritage

CONTENTS

About English Heritage	3
How to Use This Guide	4
Useful Addresses	7
Map of English Counties	8
Tour Planning Guide	9
Avon	16
Bedfordshire	17
Berkshire	19
Cambridgeshire	20
Cheshire	22
Cleveland	23
Cornwall	24
Cumbria	27
Derbyshire	31
Devon	33
Dorset	37
Durham	39
Essex	41
Gloucestershire	43
Greater London	46
Hadrian's Wall	52
Hampshire	57
Hereford and Worcester	61
Hertfordshire	63
Humberside	64
Isle of Wight	66
Isles of Scilly	68
Kent	70
Lancashire	76
Leicestershire	77
Lincolnshire	79
Norfolk	81
Northamptonshire	85
Northumberland	87
North Yorkshire	92
Nottinghamshire	97
Oxfordshire	98
Shropshire	100
Somerset	104
South Yorkshire	106
Staffordshire	108
Suffolk	109
Surrey	111
Sussex (East and West)	112
Tyne and Wear	114
Warwickshire	115
West Midlands	116
Wiltshire	117
Index	121

Front cover: Dover Castle, Kent. The vast underground military headquarters will be open to the public for the first time in May 1990 (see page 71).

Back cover (from top, left to right): Pendennis Castle, Cornwall; the Concert Bowl, Kenwood, London; living history at Helmsley Castle, North Yorkshire; Rievaulx Abbey, North Yorkshire; Boscobel House, Shropshire; Tintagel Castle, Cornwall.

Illustrations by Steve West, Adrian Knowles Associates.

Copyright © English Heritage 1990
First published 1985
Sixth (revised) edition published 1990
Design by Adrian Knowles Associates, London WC1
Printed in England by William Clowes Ltd,
Beccles, Suffolk

C1480 2/90

ISBN 1 85074 042 9

English Heritage was established by Act of Parliament in 1984. Our primary task is to care for England's great inheritance of 500,000 historic buildings and 60,000 ancient monuments. This duty covers *all* such structures, whether publicly or privately owned, and, wherever possible, their environment. Our responsibility extends to the preservation of gardens, landscapes, urban conservation areas, even machinery and ships, and the regeneration of inner cities. The scope, and the need, for our work expands constantly.

Our second function is to maintain and present to the public over 350 properties of major importance which have been entrusted to us. Prehistoric, Roman and Saxon edifices; medieval castles and monastic buildings; the fortifications of our coastline; dwellings, grand and humble, of every period, from deserted medieval villages to Queen Victoria's beloved Osborne; Stonehenge, Hadrian's Wall, Battle Abbey, Boscobel House – the whole pageant of English history is in our care.

The third, explicit, obligation of English Heritage is to *use* this glorious inheritance – for learning and teaching, for research and, above all, for enjoyment. This demands great resources of knowledge, skill and dedication, ultimately reflected in the presentation of our properties on site. *English Heritage works for everybody interested in the history and culture of England. We are determined to share our pleasures, and our responsibilities.*

Join Us!

Anybody can take part in this vital work by becoming a member of English Heritage. By paying a modest annual subscription, members gain the satisfaction of adding to the limited funds available for supporting a great national endeavour. They also derive a number of tangible, personal privileges:

* free admission to all English Heritage properties where an entrance fee is charged, and also to certain other State monuments such as the Tower of London and Hampton Court Palace

* an up-to-date copy of the *Guide to English Heritage Properties,* together with a map for expedition planning

* a quarterly magazine with all the latest news of our activities

* free or reduced admission to many events held at our properties

* reduced admission fees to historic properties in Wales and Scotland.

You can join at any staffed English Heritage property, where you will be given full details of the membership scheme so that you can enrol according to your needs. For young people there is a special section called 'Keep'.

Remember, wherever you live or go on holiday in England, you are never far from an English Heritage property!

English Heritage properties are listed in this book county-by-county (pages 15–120). If you know the name of a property but not which county it is in, refer to the alphabetical index at the back of the book. Alternatively, if you are interested in buildings or monuments of a particular period or type, a good starting point is the Tour Planning Guide on page 9.

For ease of reference there are separate chapters for properties on the Isle of Wight, the Isles of Scilly, and on Hadrian's Wall. Details of properties in the care of the Historic Royal Palaces agency (formerly the Department of the Environment) will be found in the Greater London chapter.

Property Details

Each listing in this book contains a brief description highlighting the main features of the property; directions on where to find it by road, including the National Grid reference; and details of opening times and facilities. The symbols and conventions which have been used are explained below. **Please read this section carefully.**

Opening Times

Almost all staffed properties follow the same pattern of opening, indicated by the conventions 'all year' or 'summer season'. The few exceptions to these times as stated below are noted against individual properties. *Please note that in the winter season, from 1 October to Maundy Thursday or 31 March (whichever is earlier), most properties are closed on Mondays.*

All year	Good Friday or 1 April*– 30 September *and*	Open daily 10am–6pm
	1 October–Maundy Thursday or 31 March*	Open Tuesday–Sunday 10am–4pm; closed 24–26 December and 1 January.
Summer season	Good Friday or 1 April*– 30 September	Open daily 10am–6pm.

*whichever is earlier.

Please note

1. Many properties otherwise open for the normal hours may close for lunch, usually 1–2pm.

2. In exceptional circumstances during the winter season, it may be necessary to close a property for odd days at short notice, for instance for staff training. To avoid disappointment, we strongly recommend that you telephone the property, or its Area Office (see page 7), before your visit.

3. At the properties marked 'Keykeeper', the key to the property must be obtained from a keykeeper, usually living locally. Details are usually displayed at the property itself, but can be obtained in advance of your visit by contacting the relevant Area Office (see page 7).

Admission Charges

Where there is a charge for admission to a property it is indicated by the symbol ● against the property name. Under 'admission', three prices are listed, for example 85p/65p/40p. These are the charges for:

1. adults
2. senior citizens, the unemployed (on production of a UB40) and students (on production of a student union card)
3. children under 16 (children under 5 are admitted free).

There may be an increased admission charge on days when a special event is being held at a property.

Key to Symbols

P Parking facilities at or near the property (with distance given if appropriate). For many properties where the symbol is not given, it is nevertheless possible to park easily and safely nearby. There is no charge for parking unless specified in the text.

✕ Restaurant/cafeteria available at the property (see overleaf).

🍴 Drinks and/or snacks available (usually from a vending machine).

𝛀 'Soundalive' personal stereo tour available.

⊗ No dogs please (see note below).

♿ A reasonable amount of the property may be enjoyed by visitors in wheelchairs. If access is limited to part of the site only details are given after the symbol. Toilets suitable for the disabled are listed where they are available.

Notes
1. **Dogs** are allowed in most properties; they should of course be kept under control at all times. They are not allowed in houses (apart from guide dogs), or in certain other properties, indicated by the symbol ⊗.

2. **Smoking** is not permitted in English Heritage houses.

3. **Public transport:** Many English Heritage properties are accessible by public transport. Because routes and frequency are often subject to change, details are not printed in this guide. However, details can be obtained by telephoning the property custodian (telephone numbers are given for staffed properties) or the relevant Area Office of English Heritage (see page 7).

4. **The National Trust:** Some properties listed in this Guide which are maintained and run by English Heritage are owned by the National Trust, and members of both organisations are admitted free of charge. These properties are indicated by the letters (NT) alongside the admission details.

5. **Historic Properties in Wales and Scotland:** New members of English Heritage are entitled to half-price entry to historic properties in the care of Cadw and the Scottish Development Department. After one year's membership, admission is free. For details please write to:

Friends of Scottish Monuments
SDD Room 38
20 Brandon Street
Edinburgh EH3 5RA.

Heritage in Wales
Department EH
Cadw
Brunel House
2 Fitzalan Road
Cardiff CF2 1UY.

6. **Special Events:** For a full list of special events being held at English Heritage properties in the coming year, write to the Special Events Unit, English Heritage, Keysign House, 429 Oxford Street, London W1R 2HD.

7. **London Telephone Numbers:** From 6 May 1990 the (01) code for London will be replaced by either (071) or (081). The relevant code is given after each telephone number in the Greater London chapter.

Eating Out

Your journey into England's past can be even more rewarding if you visit one of the restaurants or cafeterias at English Heritage properties. They are often set within the historic fabric of the property itself, and offer a range of hot food, snacks and drinks in atmospheric surroundings. Some even offer facilities for special functions.

The impressive restaurant and banqueting facilities at **Kenwood**, for example, are located in what was formerly the old Brew House, Laundry and Kitchen in the servants' wing, while at **Boscobel House** the stable block now contains the intimate tea rooms. Next to **Marble Hill House**, the ivy-covered Clock House Restaurant is contained within the old stable block.

Originally the housekeeper's room, the impressive restaurant at **Audley End** overlooks the spectacular grounds and the River Cam. At **Dover Castle**, you can find the spacious restaurant within the oldest part of the castle.

Both **Osborne House** and **Carisbrooke Castle** on the Isle of Wight offer attractively situated restaurants, while at **Hurst Castle** the tea room can be found in one of the castle casemates.

Next time you find yourself at one of these properties, be sure to stop for a while longer to enjoy our restaurants and cafeterias.

English ⌗ Heritage

If you have any general queries about information in this book, please contact the Marketing Division Head Office at English Heritage, Keysign House, 429 Oxford Street, London W1R 2HD.

Opening times for particular monuments may be checked either by telephoning the property itself where the number is given in this book, or by contacting the relevant Area Office at the address below.

1. Cleveland, Cumbria, Durham,
   Hadrian's Wall, Northumberland,
   Tyne and Wear

   English Heritage
   Carlisle Castle
   Carlisle CA3 8UR
   Tel. (0228) 31777

2. Cheshire, Humberside, Lancashire,
   North and South Yorkshire

   English Heritage
   Duncombe Place
   York YO1 2ED
   Tel. (0904) 658626

3. Derbyshire, Hereford and
   Worcester, Leicestershire (except
   Lyddington Bede House), Lincolnshire,
   Nottinghamshire, Shropshire,
   Staffordshire, Warwickshire,
   West Midlands

   English Heritage
   Finchfield House
   Castlecroft Road
   Wolverhampton WV3 8BY
   Tel. (0902) 765105

4. Bedfordshire, Cambridgeshire,
   Essex, Hertfordshire,
   Leicestershire (Lyddington Bede House
   only), Norfolk, Northamptonshire,
   Suffolk

   English Heritage
   24 Brooklands Avenue
   Cambridge CB2 2BU
   Tel. (0223) 455535

5. Greater London (except historic houses),
   Hampshire, Isle of Wight, Kent, Surrey,
   Sussex

   English Heritage
   Spur 17
   Government Buildings
   Hawkenbury
   Tunbridge Wells
   Kent TN2 5AQ
   Tel. (0892) 548166

6. Chiswick House, The Iveagh Bequest,
   Kenwood, Marble Hill House, Ranger's
   House

   English Heritage
   The Iveagh Bequest, Kenwood
   Hampstead Lane
   London NW3 7JR
   Tel. 01-348 1286

7. Avon, Berkshire, Cornwall, Devon,
   Dorset, Gloucestershire, Isles of Scilly,
   Oxfordshire, Somerset, Wiltshire

   English Heritage
   Bridge House
   Clifton
   Bristol BS8 4XA
   Tel. (0272) 734472

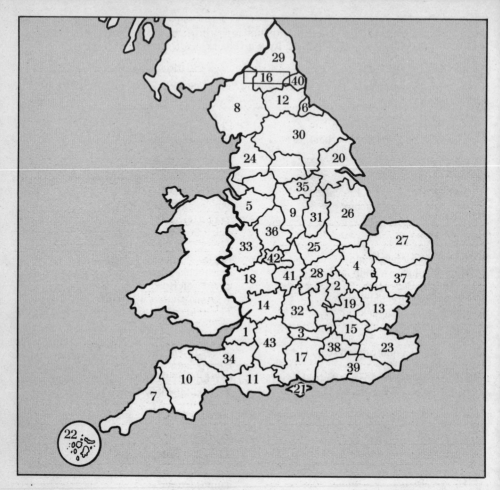

1	Avon	16	Hadrian's Wall	31	Nottinghamshire
2	Bedfordshire	17	Hampshire	32	Oxfordshire
3	Berkshire	18	Hereford and Worcester	33	Shropshire
4	Cambridgeshire	19	Hertfordshire	34	Somerset
5	Cheshire	20	Humberside	35	South Yorkshire
6	Cleveland	21	Isle of Wight	36	Staffordshire
7	Cornwall	22	Isles of Scilly	37	Suffolk
8	Cumbria	23	Kent	38	Surrey
9	Derbyshire	24	Lancashire	39	Sussex (East and West)
10	Devon	25	Leicestershire	40	Tyne and Wear
11	Dorset	26	Lincolnshire	41	Warwickshire
12	Durham	27	Norfolk	42	West Midlands
13	Essex	28	Northamptonshire	43	Wiltshire
14	Gloucestershire	29	Northumberland		
15	Greater London	30	North Yorkshire		

As an aid to tour planning, a selection of the buildings and monuments listed in this guide are classified below into categories of sites – abbeys and ecclesiastical buildings, properties with gardens, historic houses, industrial monuments, medieval castles and later fortifications, prehistoric monuments, and Roman remains. Full details of these sites are given in the county-by-county listing (see pages 15–120).

Abbeys and ecclesiastical buildings

Battle Abbey   *East Sussex*

Bayham Abbey   *East Sussex*

Binham Priory   *Norfolk*

Brinkburn Priory   *Northumberland*

Buildwas Abbey   *Shropshire*

Bury St Edmunds Abbey   *Suffolk*

Bushmead Priory   *Bedfordshire*

Byland Abbey   *North Yorkshire*

Castle Acre Priory   *Norfolk*

Chisbury Chapel   *Wiltshire*

Cleeve Abbey   *Somerset*

Creake Abbey   *Norfolk*

Croxden Abbey   *Staffordshire*

Denny Abbey   *Cambridgeshire*

Duxford Chapel   *Cambridgeshire*

Easby Abbey   *North Yorkshire*

Edvin Loach Old Church
Hereford and Worcester

Egglestone Abbey   *Durham*

Faversham Stone Chapel   *Kent*

Finchale Priory   *Durham*

Furness Abbey   *Cumbria*

Gisborough Priory   *Cleveland*

Gloucester, Blackfriars   *Gloucestershire*

Gloucester, Greyfriars   *Gloucestershire*

Goodshaw Chapel   *Lancashire*

**Greyfriars' Cloisters,
Great Yarmouth**   *Norfolk*

Hailes Abbey   *Gloucestershire*

Halesowen Abbey   *West Midlands*

Haughmond Abbey   *Shropshire*

Horne's Place Chapel, Appledore   *Kent*

Isleham Priory Church   *Cambridgeshire*

Kingswood Abbey Gatehouse
Gloucestershire

Kirkham Priory   *North Yorkshire*

Knights Templar Church, Dover   *Kent*

Lanercost Priory   *Cumbria*

Langley Chapel   *Shropshire*

Leiston Abbey   *Suffolk*

Lilleshall Abbey   *Shropshire*

Lindisfarne Priory   *Northumberland*

Mattersey Priory   *Nottinghamshire*

Milton Chantry   *Kent*

Mistley Towers   *Essex*

Monk Bretton Priory   *South Yorkshire*

Mount Grace Priory   *North Yorkshire*

Muchelney Abbey   *Somerset*

Netley Abbey   *Hampshire*

North Elmham Cathedral   *Norfolk*

Odda's Chapel, Deerhurst   *Gloucestershire*

Old Sarum (Cathedral and Bishop's Palace)   *Wiltshire*

Portsmouth Garrison Church   *Hampshire*

Reculver Towers   *Kent*

Rievaulx Abbey   *North Yorkshire*

Roche Abbey   *South Yorkshire*

Rotherwas Chapel   *Hereford and Worcester*

Rufford Abbey   *Nottinghamshire*

Rycote Chapel   *Oxfordshire*

St Augustine's Abbey, Canterbury   *Kent*

St Botolph's Priory, Colchester   *Essex*

St James's Chapel, Lindsey   *Suffolk*

St Mary's Church, Kempley   *Gloucestershire*

St Olave's Priory   *Norfolk*

St Paul's Monastery, Jarrow   *Tyne and Wear*

St Peter's Church, Barton-upon-Humber   *Humberside*

Salley Abbey   *Lancashire*

Shap Abbey   *Cumbria*

Studley Royal: St Mary's Church   *North Yorkshire*

Temple Church, Bristol   *Avon*

Thetford: Church of the Holy Sepulchre   *Norfolk*

Thetford Priory   *Norfolk*

Thornton Abbey   *Humberside*

Titchfield Abbey   *Hampshire*

Tynemouth Priory   *Tyne and Wear*

Waltham Abbey Gatehouse   *Essex*

Warkworth Hermitage   *Northumberland*

Waverley Abbey   *Surrey*

Wenlock Priory   *Shropshire*

Westminster Abbey Chapter House and Pyx Chamber   *Greater London*

Wetheral Priory Gatehouse   *Cumbria*

Wharram Percy Church   *North Yorkshire*

Whitby Abbey   *North Yorkshire*

White Ladies Priory   *Shropshire*

Gardens

Appuldurcombe House   *Isle of Wight*

Audley End House and Park   *Essex*

Belsay Hall, Castle and Gardens   *Northumberland*

Boscobel House   *Shropshire*

Chiswick House   *Greater London*

Hampton Court Palace   *Greater London*

Kenwood House   *Greater London*

Kew Palace   *Greater London*

Kirby Hall   *Northamptonshire*

Marble Hill House   *Greater London*

Old Wardour Castle   *Wiltshire*

Osborne House   *Isle of Wight*

St Mawes Castle   *Cornwall*

Walmer Castle   *Kent*

Wrest Park House and Gardens   *Bedfordshire*

Historic houses

Acton Burnell Castle   *Shropshire*

Appuldurcombe House   *Isle of Wight*

Audley End House and Park   *Essex*

Banqueting House, Whitehall   *Greater London*

Belsay Hall   *Northumberland*

Bessie Surtees House   *Tyne and Wear*

Bishop's Palace, Lincoln   *Lincolnshire*

Bishop's Waltham Palace   *Hampshire*

Bolsover Castle   *Derbyshire*

Boscobel House   *Shropshire*

Burton Agnes Manor House   *Humberside*

Chiswick House   *Greater London*

Christchurch Norman House   *Dorset*

Clifton Hall   *Cumbria*

Eltham Palace   *Greater London*

Fiddleford Manor   *Dorset*

Gainsborough Old Hall   *Lincolnshire*

Glastonbury Tribunal   *Somerset*

The Grange, Northington   *Hampshire*

Hampton Court Palace   *Greater London*

Hardwick Old Hall   *Derbyshire*

Houghton House   *Bedfordshire*

Jewel Tower, Westminster   *Greater London*

Kensington Palace   *Greater London*

Kenwood   *Greater London*

Kew Palace   *Greater London*

Kirby Hall   *Northamptonshire*

Kirkham House, Paignton   *Devon*

Longthorpe Tower   *Cambridgeshire*

Lyddington Bede House   *Leicestershire*

Maison Dieu   *Kent*

Marble Hill House   *Greater London*

Minster Lovell Hall and Dovecot   *Oxfordshire*

Moreton Corbet Castle   *Shropshire*

Old Gorhambury House   *Hertfordshire*

Old Merchant's House and Row 111 Houses   *Norfolk*

Old Soar Manor, Plaxtol   *Kent*

Osborne House   *Isle of Wight*

Ranger's House   *Greater London*

Rushton Triangular Lodge   *Northamptonshire*

Southampton: Medieval Merchant's House   *Hampshire*

Stokesay Castle   *Shropshire*

Sutton Scarsdale Hall   *Derbyshire*

Temple Manor, Rochester   *Kent*

Thetford Warren Lodge   *Norfolk*

Winchester Palace   *Greater London*

Witley Court   *Hereford and Worcester*

Wolvesey   *Hampshire*

Wrest Park House and Gardens   *Bedfordshire*

Industrial monuments

Berney Arms Windmill   *Norfolk*

Cantlop Bridge   *Shropshire*

Coombe Conduit   *Surrey*

Iron Bridge   *Shropshire*

Mortimers' Cross Water Mill   *Hereford and Worcester*

Over Bridge   *Gloucestershire*

Saxtead Green Post Mill   *Suffolk*

Sibsey Trader Windmill   *Lincolnshire*

Stott Park Bobbin Mill   *Cumbria*

Medieval castles and later fortifications

Ashby de la Zouch Castle   *Leicestershire*

Aydon Castle   *Northumberland*

Baconsthorpe Castle   *Norfolk*

Barnard Castle   *Durham*

Bayard's Cove Fort, Dartmouth   *Devon*

Beeston Castle   *Cheshire*

Belsay Castle   *Northumberland*

Berkhamsted Castle   *Hertfordshire*

Berry Pomeroy Castle   *Devon*

Berwick-upon-Tweed Castle and Ramparts   *Northumberland*

Black Middens Bastle House   *Northumberland*

Bolingbroke Castle   *Lincolnshire*

Bowes Castle   *Durham*

Bramber Castle   *West Sussex*

Brougham Castle   *Cumbria*

Brough Castle   *Cumbria*

Calshot Castle   *Hampshire*

Carisbrooke Castle   *Isle of Wight*

Carlisle Castle   *Cumbria*

Castle Acre Castle   *Norfolk*

Castle Rising Castle   *Norfolk*

Chester Castle: Agricola Tower and Castle Walls   *Cheshire*

Christchurch Castle   *Dorset*

Clifford's Tower, York   *North Yorkshire*

Conisbrough Castle   *South Yorkshire*

Cromwell's Castle   *Isles of Scilly*

Dartmouth Castle   *Devon*

Deal Castle   *Kent*

Deddington Castle   *Oxfordshire*

Donnington Castle   *Berkshire*

Dover Castle   *Kent*

Dunstanburgh Castle   *Northumberland*

Dymchurch Martello Tower   *Kent*

Edlingham Castle   *Northumberland*

Etal Castle   *Northumberland*

Eynsford Castle   *Kent*

Farleigh Hungerford Castle   *Somerset*

Farnham Castle Keep   *Surrey*

Fort Brockhurst   *Hampshire*

Framlingham Castle   *Suffolk*

Goodrich Castle   *Hereford and Worcester*

Hadleigh Castle   *Essex*

Helmsley Castle   *North Yorkshire*

Hurst Castle   *Hampshire*

Hylton Castle   *Tyne and Wear*

Kenilworth Castle   *Warwickshire*

Kirby Muxloe Castle   *Leicestershire*

Launceston Castle   *Cornwall*

Longtown Castle   *Hereford and Worcester*

Ludgershall Castle   *Wiltshire*

Lydford Castles and Saxon Town   *Devon*

Middleham Castle   *North Yorkshire*

Moreton Corbet Castle   *Shropshire*

Norham Castle   *Northumberland*

Nunney Castle   *Somerset*

Okehampton Castle   *Devon*

Old Sarum   *Wiltshire*

Old Wardour Castle   *Wiltshire*

Orford Castle   *Suffolk*

Pendennis Castle   *Cornwall*

Penrith Castle   *Cumbria*

Pevensey Castle   *East Sussex*

Peveril Castle   *Derbyshire*

Pickering Castle   *North Yorkshire*

Piel Castle   *Cumbria*

Portchester Castle   *Hampshire*

Portland Castle   *Dorset*

Prudhoe Castle   *Northumberland*

Restormel Castle   *Cornwall*

Richmond Castle   *North Yorkshire*

Rochester Castle   *Kent*

St Mawes Castle   *Cornwall*

Scarborough Castle   *North Yorkshire*

Sherborne Old Castle   *Dorset*

Skipsea Castle   *Humberside*

Spofforth Castle   *North Yorkshire*

Stokesay Castle   *Shropshire*

Sutton Valence Castle   *Kent*

Tilbury Fort   *Essex*

Tintagel Castle   *Cornwall*

Totnes Castle   *Devon*

Tower of London   *Greater London*

Tynemouth Castle   *Tyne and Wear*

Upnor Castle   *Kent*

Walmer Castle   *Kent*

Warkworth Castle   *Northumberland*

Weeting Castle   *Norfolk*

Yarmouth Castle   *Isle of Wight*

Prehistoric monuments

Arbor Low Stone Circle and
Gib Hill Barrow   *Derbyshire*

Arthur's Round Table   *Cumbria*

Arthur's Stone, Dorstone
Hereford and Worcester

Avebury Stone Circles   *Wiltshire*

Ballowall Barrow, St Just   *Cornwall*

Bant's Carn Burial Chamber and Halangy
Down Ancient Village
Isles of Scilly

Belas Knap Long Barrow   *Gloucestershire*

Blackbury Camp   *Devon*

Bratton Camp and White Horse   *Wiltshire*

Carn Euny Ancient Village   *Cornwall*

Castlerigg Stone Circle   *Cumbria*

Chysauster Ancient Village   *Cornwall*

Flowerdown Barrows   *Hampshire*

Grime's Graves   *Norfolk*

Grimspound   *Devon*

Halliggye Fogou   *Cornwall*

Hob Hurst's House   *Derbyshire*

Hurler's Stone Circle   *Cornwall*

Innisidgen Lower and Upper
Burial Chambers   *Isles of Scilly*

Kingston Russell Stone Circle   *Dorset*

Kit's Coty House and Little Kit's
Coty House   *Kent*

Maiden Castle   *Dorset*

Mayburgh Earthwork   *Cumbria*

Merrivale Prehistoric Settlement   *Devon*

Mitchell's Fold Stone Circle   *Shropshire*

Nine Ladies Stone Circle, Stanton Moor
Derbyshire

The Nine Stones, Winterbourne Abbas
Dorset

Nympsfield Long Barrow   *Gloucestershire*

Old Sarum   *Wiltshire*

Old Oswestry Hill Fort   *Shropshire*

Porth Hellick Down Burial
Chamber   *Isles of Scilly*

St Breock Downs Monolith   *Cornwall*

The Sanctuary, Overton Hill,
Avebury   *Wiltshire*

Silbury Hill, Avebury   *Wiltshire*

Stanton Drew Stone Circles and
Cove   *Avon*

Stonehenge   *Wiltshire*

Stoney Littleton Long Barrow   *Avon*

Tregiffian Burial Chamber,
St Buryan   *Cornwall*

Trethevy Quoit, St Cleer   *Cornwall*

Uffington Castle, White Horse and
Dragon Hill   *Oxfordshire*

Uley Long Barrow   *Gloucestershire*

Upper Plym Valley   *Devon*

Wayland's Smithy   *Oxfordshire*

West Kennet Avenue, Avebury   *Wiltshire*

West Kennet Long Barrow   *Wiltshire*

Windmill Hill, Avebury   *Wiltshire*

Windmill Tump Long Barrow,
Rodmarton   *Gloucestershire*

Winterbourne Poor Lot Barrows   *Dorset*

Woodhenge   *Wiltshire*

Roman remains

Aldborough Roman Town   *North Yorkshire*

Ambleside Roman Fort   *Cumbria*

Bank's East Turret   *Hadrian's Wall*

Benwell Roman Temple and Vallum Crossing   *Hadrian's Wall*

Birdoswald Fort, Wall and Turret   *Hadrian's Wall*

Black Carts Turret   *Hadrian's Wall*

Brunton Turret   *Hadrian's Wall*

Burgh Castle   *Norfolk*

Caister Roman Site   *Norfolk*

Carrawburgh Temple of Mithras   *Hadrian's Wall*

Cawfields Roman Wall and Milecastle *Hadrian's Wall*

Chester Roman Amphitheatre   *Cheshire*

Chesters Bridge Abutment   *Hadrian's Wall*

Chesters Fort   *Hadrian's Wall*

Cirencester Amphitheatre   *Gloucestershire*

Corbridge Roman Site   *Hadrian's Wall*

Denton Hall Turret and West Denton   *Hadrian's Wall*

Faversham Stone Chapel   *Kent*

Gilsland Vicarage Roman Wall   *Cumbria*

Great Witcombe Roman Villa *Gloucestershire*

Hardknott Roman Fort   *Cumbria*

Hare Hill   *Hadrian's Wall*

Harrow's Scar Milecastle   *Hadrian's Wall*

Heddon-on-the-Wall   *Hadrian's Wall*

Housesteads Roman Fort   *Hadrian's Wall*

Jewry Wall, Leicester   *Leicestershire*

Jordan Hill Roman Temple, Weymouth   *Dorset*

Leahill Turret   *Hadrian's Wall*

Lullingstone Roman Villa   *Kent*

North Leigh Roman Villa   *Oxfordshire*

Piercebridge Roman Bridge *North Yorkshire*

Pike Hill Signal Tower   *Hadrian's Wall*

Piper Sike Turret   *Hadrian's Wall*

Planetrees Roman Wall   *Hadrian's Wall*

Poltross Burn Milecastle   *Hadrian's Wall*

Ravenglass Roman Bath House   *Cumbria*

Reculver Roman Fort   *Kent*

Richborough Castle   *Kent*

Richborough Roman Amphitheatre   *Kent*

St Albans Roman Wall   *Hertfordshire*

Sewingshields Wall, Turrets and Milecastle   *Hadrian's Wall*

Silchester Roman City Wall   *Hampshire*

Vindolanda Fort and Roman Milestone *Hadrian's Wall*

Wall Roman Site   *Staffordshire*

Walltown Crags Wall and Turret   *Hadrian's Wall*

Wheeldale Roman Road   *North Yorkshire*

Willowford Bridge Abutment *Hadrian's Wall*

Winshields Wall and Milecastle *Hadrian's Wall*

Wroxeter Roman City   *Shropshire*

County-by-County
Guide

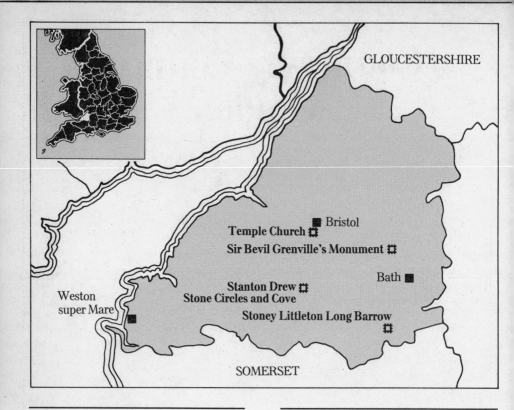

Map showing locations in Avon: GLOUCESTERSHIRE, Bristol, Temple Church, Sir Bevil Grenville's Monument, Bath, Weston super Mare, Stanton Drew Stone Circles and Cove, Stoney Littleton Long Barrow, SOMERSET

Bristol: Temple Church
In Temple St off Victoria St
Walls and tower of 15th-century church
bombed in World War II, which stands on
the site of a 12th-century Knights
Templar church.
Open: Any reasonable time (exterior
viewing only).
Facilities: &
OS Map 172; ref ST 593727

Sir Bevil Grenville's Monument, Lansdown
*4m NW of Bath, on N edge of Lansdown
Hill, near road to Wick*
Early 18th-century monument to Sir
Bevil Grenville, slain at the battle of
Lansdown, 1643.
Open: Any reasonable time.
OS Map 172; ref ST 721703

Stanton Drew Circles and Cove
*Circles: E of Stanton Drew village;
Cove: In garden of the Druid's Arms*
One of the finest Neolithic monuments
of its type in the country, which consists of
three stone circles, two avenues of standing
stones and a burial chamber.
Open: Any reasonable time but closed
Sun. NB access via private land: the owner
may levy a charge on all visitors.
OS Map 172; Circles ref ST 601634,
Cove ref ST 598633

Stoney Littleton Long Barrow
1m S of Wellow off A367
Neolithic chambered burial mound, with
central passage built with dry-stone
walls and roof slabs, and lateral
recesses for human remains.
Open: Any reasonable time.
OS Map 172; ref ST 735573

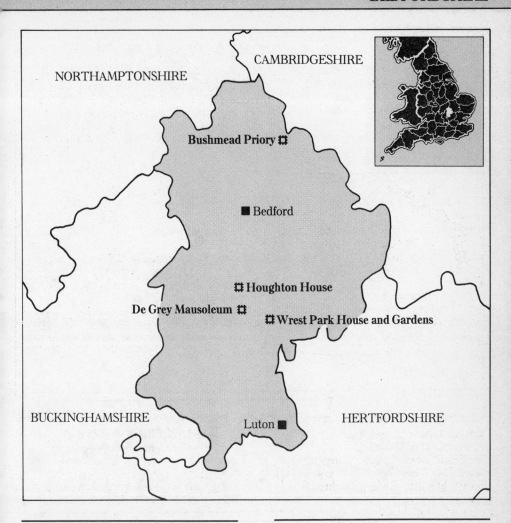

NORTHAMPTONSHIRE

CAMBRIDGESHIRE

Bushmead Priory ⌘

■ Bedford

⌘ **Houghton House**

De Grey Mausoleum ⌘

⌘ **Wrest Park House and Gardens**

BUCKINGHAMSHIRE

HERTFORDSHIRE

Luton ■

● **Bushmead Priory**
On unclassified road near Colmworth,
2m E of B660
Medieval refectory of Augustinian priory,
with rare timber-frame roof of crown-post
construction. Contains wall paintings and
interesting stained glass. Site display.
Open: Summer season, weekends only,
Sat 10am–6pm, Sun 2pm–6pm. 85p/65p/40p.
Facilities: 🅿
Tel: (023062) 614
OS Map 153; ref TL 115607

Bushmead Priory

De Grey Mausoleum
Flitton, attached to church, on unclassified road 1½m W of A6 at Silsoe
Mausoleum of the de Grey family of Wrest Park, containing a magnificent collection of monuments from the 16th to 19th centuries.
Open: Any reasonable time. Keykeeper. Mr JAM Stimson, 3 Highfield Road, Flitton.
OS Map 153; ref TL 059359

Houghton House
1m NE of Ampthill off A418, 8m S of Bedford
Remains of an early 17th-century mansion built for Mary, Countess of Pembroke and with work attributed to Inigo Jones. Commonly identified with the 'House Beautiful' in Bunyan's 'Pilgrim's Progress'.
Open: Any reasonable time.
Facilities: P &
OS Map 153; ref TL 039394

● Wrest Park House and Gardens
¾m E of Silsoe off A6
Formal gardens laid out for the Duke of Kent in the early 18th century, later partly remodelled by 'Capability' Brown and others. Principal rooms on ground floor of House, built 1834–39 in French style, also open to the public.
Open: Summer season, weekends & Bank Holidays only 10am–6pm.
£1.15/85p/60p.
Facilities: Toilets P ✕ ⊗
Tel: (0525) 60718
OS Map 153; ref TL 093356

Wrest Park: Bowling Green House, Gardens

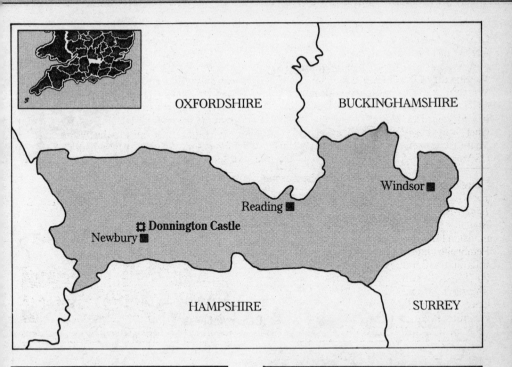

Donnington Castle

1m N of Newbury off A34
Built late 14th century, the twin-towered gatehouse survives, with earthworks from the Civil War period, when the castle underwent a long siege (1644–46).
Open: Any reasonable time.
Facilities: ▣ (car park closes 6.30pm)
♿ (steep slopes within grounds)
OS Map 174; ref SU 461694

Opening times

All year

Good Friday or 1 April* – 30 Sept:
Open daily 10am-6pm

1 Oct-Maundy Thursday or 31 March*:
Open daily 10am-4pm;
closed Mondays, 24-26 Dec, 1 Jan.

Summer season

Good Friday or 1 April* – 30 Sept:
Open daily 10am-6pm.

*whichever is earlier

LINCOLNSHIRE

NORTHAMPTON-
SHIRE

Peterborough
Longthorpe Tower

NORFOLK

Ely ■

Isleham Priory Church ⊞

Denny Abbey ⊞

SUFFOLK

Cambridge ■

Duxford Chapel ⊞

BEDFORDSHIRE

ESSEX

● **Denny Abbey**
6m N of Cambridge on A10
Roofed remains of 12th-century Benedictine
abbey, later adapted and occupied in turn by
the Knights Templar and Franciscan nuns,
who built the 14th-century dining hall.
Open: Summer season, daily;
Sundays only in winter, 10am–4pm.
85p/65p/40p.
Facilities: **P** & (grounds & ground floor only)
Tel: (0223) 860489
OS Map 154; ref TL 495684

Denny Abbey

Duxford Chapel
*Adjacent to Whittlesford station
off A505*
14th-century chapel with interesting
detail, once part of the Hospital of St John.
Open: Any reasonable time. Keykeeper.
OS Map 154; ref TL 486472

Isleham Priory Church
*In Isleham, 23m NE of Cambridge on
B1104*
Apsidal Norman church of *c.*1100 with
much 'herringbone' masonry. Little altered
despite later conversion to barn.
Open: Any reasonable time. Keykeeper.
OS Map 143; ref TL 642744

● Longthorpe Tower
2m W of Peterborough on A47
14th-century tower of manor house. The
wall paintings on the first floor, with
Biblical and domestic scenes, form the most
complete set of such paintings of the
period in England. Changing special
exhibitions.
Open: All year. 85p/65p/40p.
Tel: (0733) 268482
OS Map 142; ref TL 163983

Longthorpe Tower

Music through the Ages

From April to October 1990 our
musical duo 'Hautbois' will once
again entertain visitors at numer-
ous properties with Medieval and Renaissance
music. As well as supporting major events
and touring castles in their own right, they
will present informal programmes of religious
and secular music at abbeys and priories,
including Castle Acre and Wenlock Priories,
Bishop's Waltham Palace, plus Cleeve, Netley
and Bayham Abbeys.

English ⌗ Heritage

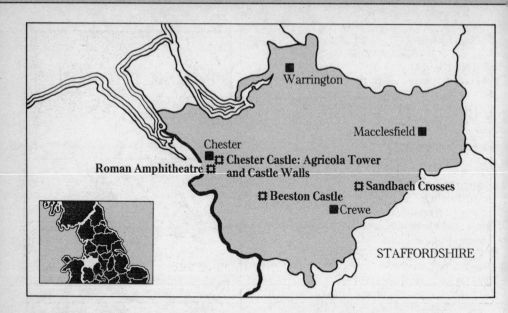

STAFFORDSHIRE

● **Beeston Castle**
11m SE of Chester on minor road off A49
Dramatically sited ruins, including the
inner and outer wards, of castle begun
in 1220. From the inner ward there are
spectacular views of the surrounding
countryside. Exhibition on the history of
the castle.
Open: All year. £1.40/£1.05/70p.
Facilities: Toilets ℗
Tel: (0829) 260464
OS Map 117; ref SJ 537593

Beeston Castle

**Chester Castle: Agricola Tower and
Castle Walls**
*Access via Assizes Court car park
on Grosvenor St*
12th-century tower containing a fine
vaulted chapel. Exhibition in
19th-century Guard Room.
Open: All year.
Facilities: ♿ (parts)
OS Map 117: ref SJ 405658

Chester Roman Amphitheatre
On Vicars Lane beyond Newgate, Chester
Partially excavated amphitheatre of
Deva, the fortress of the 20th Legion.
Open: All year.
Facilities: ♿ (no access to
Amphitheatre floor)
OS Map 117; ref SJ 404660

Sandbach Crosses
Market Square, Sandbach
9th-century stone crosses with carved
ornament and figures. Further carved Saxon
stones outside nearby church.
Open: Any reasonable time.
Facilities: ♿
OS Map 118; ref SJ 758608

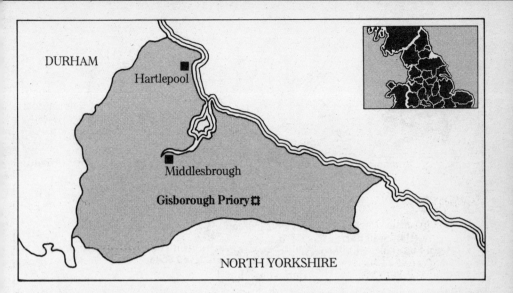

DURHAM

Hartlepool

Middlesbrough

Gisborough Priory ⌗

NORTH YORKSHIRE

● **Gisborough Priory**
In Guisborough town, next to parish church
Augustinian priory founded in the first
half of the 12th century. Remains
include 12th-century gatehouse and fine
east end of early 14th-century church.
Open: All year. 60p/45p/30p.
Facilities: &
Tel: (0287) 38301
OS Map 94; ref NZ 618163

Gisborough Priory

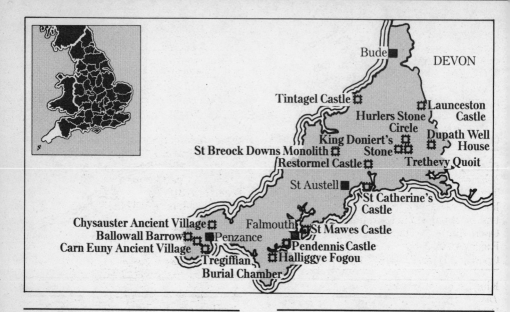

Ballowall Barrow, St Just
1m W of St Just, near Carn Gloose
A Bronze Age chambered tomb of unusual type; in use *c*.1400–600BC.
Open: Any reasonable time.
OS Map 203; ref SW 354313

Carn Euny Ancient Village
1¼m SW of Sancreed off A30
Remains of an Iron Age settlement built before 500BC and inhabited well into the 1st century AD. Small site exhibition.
Open: Any reasonable time.
Facilities: P
OS Map 203; ref SW 402289

● Chysauster Ancient Village
2½m NW of Gulval off B3311
Romano-Cornish village of the 2nd and 3rd century AD, probably on a late Iron Age site, consisting of a number of stone houses. Each contains a number of rooms around an open court.
Open: All year. 85p/65p/40p.
Facilities: Toilets P
Tel: (0736) 61889
OS Map 203; ref SW 473350

Dupath Well House, Callington
1m E of Callington off A388
An almost complete well house built over a holy well, *c*.1500.
Open: Any reasonable time.
OS Map 201; ref SX 374693

Chysauster Ancient Village

Halliggye Fogou

*5m SE of Helston off B3293 E of Garras
on Trelowarren estate*
An underground chamber normally
associated with Iron Age open villages,
possibly used for refuge or food storage.
Open: Any reasonable time.
A torch is advisable.
OS Map 203; ref SW 714239

Hurlers Stone Circle

½m NW of Minions off B3254
Three Bronze Age stone circles in a
line; one of the best examples of this
type of monument in the south-west.
Open: Any reasonable time.
Facilities: ▣(lay-by)
OS Map 201; ref SX 258714

King Doniert's Stone, St Cleer

1m NW of St Cleer off B3254
Part of a decorated cross-shaft
inscribed 'DONIERT ROGAVIT PRO
ANIMA'. Doniert was probably Durngarth,
King of Cornwall, who drowned *c.*AD875.
Open: Any reasonable time.
OS Map 201; ref SX 236688

● Launceston Castle

In Launceston
Fine castle founded by Robert of Mortain,
brother of William I. Existing remains,
mainly 12th- and 13th-century, include a
walled bailey and a cylindrical keep
on top of a high mound. Site exhibition.
Open: All year. 85p/65p/40p.
Facilities: & (outer bailey)
Tel: (0566) 2365
OS Map 201; ref SX 330846

Launceston Castle

● Pendennis Castle

On Pendennis Head 1m SE of Falmouth
Well-preserved example of the coastal
forts erected by Henry VIII to counter
the threat of invasion, surrounded by
late 16th-century fortifications. During
the Civil War it was captured by
the Parliamentary Army after a 5 months'
siege. Exhibition and gun deck display.
Open: All year. £1.40/£1.05/70p.
Facilities: Toilets ▣ ☕ 🎧 ⊗
& (grounds, part keep)
Tel: (0326) 316594
OS Map 204; ref SW 824318

Pendennis Castle

● Restormel Castle

1½m N of Lostwithiel off A390
Picturesquely sited Norman ringwork,
the walls on the motte forming a large,
circular shell-keep of *c.*1200.
Open: All year. 85p/65p/40p.
Facilities: Toilets ▣
Tel: (020887) 2687
OS Map 200; ref SX 104614

Restormel Castle

St Breock Downs Monolith
*On St Breock Downs, 3¾m SSW of
Wadebridge off A39*
A longstone of prehistoric date
originally about 16ft high.
Open: Any reasonable time.
OS Map 200; ref SW 968683

St Catherine's Castle, Fowey
¾m SW of Fowey off A3082
A fort erected in the reign of Henry
VIII for the defence of the harbour.
Open: Any reasonable time.
OS Map 200; ref SX 118508

● St Mawes Castle
In St Mawes on A3078
One of two coastal forts built by Henry
VIII to defend the Fal estuary. The unusual
clover-leaf plan is produced by a central
tower with three semi-circular bastions.
Open: All year. 85p/65p/40p.
Facilities: Toilets ℗ ⊗
& (grounds & ground floor only)
Tel: (0326) 270526
OS Map 204; ref SW 842328

St Mawes Castle

● Tintagel Castle
*On Tintagel Head, along track from
Tintagel (no vehicles)*
Remains of medieval castle founded in
the 12th century by Reginald, Earl of
Cornwall on a Dark Age settlement site
and now divided into two parts by sea
erosion. Small site exhibition.
Open: All year. £1.40/£1.05/70p.
Facilities: Souvenir shop, toilets ℗ (in
Tintagel village) ☞
Tel: (0840) 770328
OS Map 200; ref SX 048891

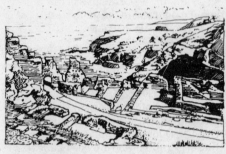

Tintagel Castle

Tregiffian Burial Chamber, St Buryan
2m SE of St Buryan on B3315
Neolithic/Early Bronze Age chambered
tomb.
Open: Any reasonable time.
OS Map 203; ref SW 430245

Trethevy Quoit, St Cleer
1m NE of St Cleer off B3254
Neolithic burial chamber consisting of
five standing stones surmounted by a huge
capstone, once covered by an earthen
mound and probably built before 2000BC.
Open: Any reasonable time.
OS Map 201; ref SX 259688

**For full details of
opening times see page 4**

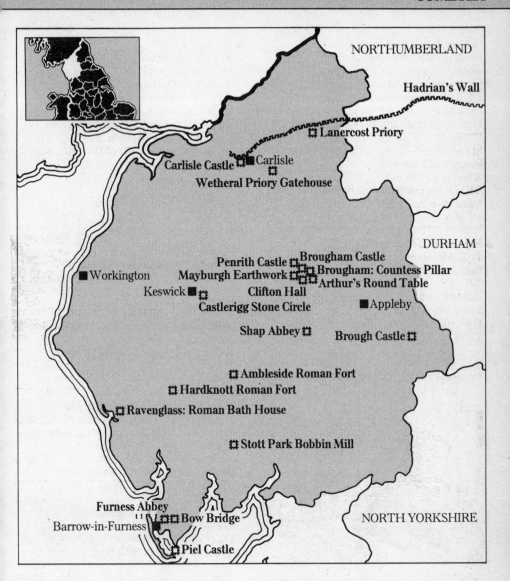

NORTHUMBERLAND

Hadrian's Wall

Lanercost Priory

Carlisle Castle ▦ Carlisle
Wetheral Priory Gatehouse

DURHAM

Penrith Castle ▦ Brougham Castle
■ Workington   Mayburgh Earthwork ▦ Brougham: Countess Pillar
Keswick ▦   Arthur's Round Table
Clifton Hall
Castlerigg Stone Circle   ■ Appleby

Shap Abbey ▦
Brough Castle ▦

▦ Ambleside Roman Fort
▦ Hardknott Roman Fort
▦ Ravenglass: Roman Bath House

▦ Stott Park Bobbin Mill

Furness Abbey
Barrow-in-Furness ▦ Bow Bridge   NORTH YORKSHIRE

▦ Piel Castle

Ambleside Roman Fort
200yd W of Waterhead car park, Ambleside
Remains of the Roman fort of Galava,
founded in the 1st century AD to guard
the road between Ravenglass and
Brougham.
Open: Any reasonable time. (NT)
OS Map 90; ref NY 376033

Arthur's Round Table
At Eamont Bridge, 1m S of Penrith
A prehistoric earthwork consisting of
a roughly circular area bounded by
a ditch with a bank on the outside.
Open: Any reasonable time.
Facilities: ♿
OS Map 90; ref NY 523284

Bow Bridge, Barrow-in-Furness

*1/2m N of Barrow-in-Furness, on
minor road off A590 near Furness Abbey*
Late medieval stone bridge across the
Mill Beck, carrying a route connected
with Furness Abbey.
Open: Any reasonable time.
OS Map 96; ref SD 224715

● Brougham Castle

1 1/2m SE of Penrith
Impressive remains, which include a keep
dating from the early 13th century
and later buildings set round a paved
courtyard. The Castle was restored by
Lady Anne Clifford in the 17th century.
Small exhibition of Roman tombstones from
cemetery of nearby Roman fort.
Open: All year. 85p/65p/40p.
Facilities: ▣ & (excluding keep)
Tel: (0768) 62488
OS Map 90; ref NY 537290

Brougham Castle

Brougham: Countess Pillar

1m SE of Brougham on A66
Pillar, bearing a bronze inscription
and sundials, set up in 1656 by Lady
Anne Clifford to commemorate her
parting with her mother in 1616.
Open: Any reasonable time.
OS Map 90; ref NY 546289

● Brough Castle

8m SE of Appleby S of A66
12th-century keep and enclosure walls
on the site of a Roman fort replacing an
earlier stronghold destroyed by the
Scots in 1174. The Castle was restored
by Lady Anne Clifford in the 17th century.
Open: All year. 60p/45p/30p.
OS Map 91; ref NY 791141

Brough Castle

● Carlisle Castle

N of Carlisle town centre
Impressive medieval castle at a key point
on the Anglo-Scottish border. Mary Queen
of Scots was imprisoned here. Surviving
buildings include inner and outer wards
enclosing a 12th-century keep with
panoramic views. Exhibition; model of the
city *c.*1745; Museum of the King's Own
Border Regiment. Furnished suite of
medieval rooms in outer gatehouse. Living
history centre. Souvenir shop.
Open: All year, plus Mondays in winter.
£1.40/£1.05/70p.
Facilities: Toilets ☛ ▣ (disabled only)
& (except interiors of buildings)
Tel: (0228) 31777
OS Map 85; ref NY 397563

Carlisle Castle

Castlerigg Stone Circle
1½m E of Keswick
Stone circle of Neolithic or Bronze Age
date in a superb Lakeland landscape
setting.
Open: Any reasonable time. (NT)
OS Map 90; ref NY 293236

Clifton Hall
*In Clifton next to Clifton Hall
Farm, 2m S of Penrith on A6*
15th-century tower block, the surviving
domestic rooms of the manor of Clifton,
and once part of a complex of buildings.
Open: All year.
OS Map 90; ref NY 530271

● Furness Abbey
*1½m N of Barrow-in-Furness, on minor
road off A590*
Extensive remains, in a beautiful
setting, of the abbey founded in 1123
by Stephen, (later King of England),
which belonged first to the Order of
Savigny and later the Cistercians. Site
museum and exhibition.
Open: All year. £1.40/£1.05/70p (includes
free audio tour).
Facilities: Toilets 🅿 🍴 🎧 ♿
Tel: (0229) 23420
OS Map 96; ref SD 218717

Hadrian's Wall
See pages 52–56

Hardknott Roman Fort
*9m NE of Ravenglass, at W end of
Hardknott Pass*
A fort of some 2¾ acres built at a date
between AD120 and 138, on spectacular
site overlooking the pass from Ravenglass
to Ambleside. Visible remains include
granaries, headquarters building, the
commandant's house, with a bath house
and parade ground outside the fort.
Open: Any reasonable time. Access
may be hazardous in winter.
Facilities: 🅿
OS Map 96; ref NY 218015

● Lanercost Priory
*Off minor road S of Lanercost, 2m NE of
Brampton*
Augustinian priory founded *c.*1166.
The nave of the church, intact and still
in use, contrasts with the ruined chancel,
transepts and priory buildings.
Open: Summer season. 60p/45p/30p.
Facilities: 🅿 ♿
Tel: (06977) 3030
OS Map 86; NY 556637

Furness Abbey

Lanercost Priory

Mayburgh Earthwork
At Eamont Bridge, 1m S of Penrith off A6
Impressive prehistoric monument,
consisting of a ring-bank of stones around
a central area containing a single large
stone, the remnant of a stone circle.
Open: Any reasonable time.
OS Map 90; ref NY 519285

Penrith Castle
Opposite Penrith railway station
14th-century castle, built round a
courtyard and built to defend the town
from repeated attacks by Scottish raiders.
Open: Park opening hours.
Facilities: Toilets
OS Map 90; ref NY 513299

Piel Castle
On Piel Island, 3¼m SE of Barrow
Ruins of 14th-century castle of the
abbots of Furness, with massive keep
and inner and outer baileys defended by
curtain walls and towers. Restricted access
during consolidation works.
Open: Any reasonable time. Access by
ferry from Roa Island: summer weekdays
from 11am subject to tides. Winter by
arrangement, tel. (0229) 22520 weekdays,
(0229) 21741 weekends.
OS Map 96; ref SD 233636

Ravenglass: Roman Bath House
*¼m E of Ravenglass, off minor road
leading to A595*
Standing remains of bath house originally
belonging to the Roman fort at Ravenglass.
Open: Any reasonable time.
OS Map 96; ref NY 088961

Shap Abbey
1½m W of Shap on bank of River Lowther
Premonstratensian abbey founded *c.*1180
at Preston Patrick and moved to Shap
*c.*1199. Most of the buildings are
13th-century, but a striking surviving
feature is the early 16th-century west tower.
Open: Any reasonable time.
Facilities: ⊞ &
OS Map 90; ref NY 548153

● Stott Park Bobbin Mill
½m N of Finsthwaite near Newby Bridge
Built in 1835 and virtually unchanged
for 150 years, the mill has been
restored as a working industrial
monument. Much of the machinery still
remains, including a turbine and steam
engine. Visitors are conducted through
the mill by a guide. Exhibition.
Open: Summer season (closes at dusk if
before 6pm). £1.40/£1.05/70p.
Facilities: Toilets ⊞ & (ground floor only)
Tel: (0448) 31087
OS Map 96; ref SD 373883

Stott Park Bobbin Mill

Wetheral Priory Gatehouse
*On minor road in Wetheral village,
6m E of Carlisle on B6263*
Small 15th-century gatehouse of a
Benedictine priory founded in 1106, and
comprising mainly domestic apartments.
Open: All year.
OS Map 86; ref NY 468542

**Arbor Low Stone Circle and
Gib Hill Barrow**
1/2m W of A515 2m S of Monyash
Fine Neolithic henge monument, consisting
of an unusually large ditch and bank
surrounding an oval setting of stones, which
were overturned in antiquity. Nearby
is Gib Hill Barrow.
Open: Any reasonable time. (The farmer
who owns the right of way to the site
may levy a charge.)
OS Map 119; ref SK 161636

Bolsover Castle

In Bolsover, 6m E of Chesterfield on A632
Early 17th-century house of exuberant
architectural style, in castle form,
designed by Robert and John Smythson for
the Cavendish family. The family suite in
the self-contained 'keep' is richly decorated
with allegorical paintings and carved
fireplaces. There is a state range, now
roofless, and one of the earliest indoor
riding schools. Displays in keep and
riding school master's lodge.
Open: All year. £1.40/£1.05/70p.
Facilities: Toilets **P** & (except keep)
Tel: (0246) 823349
OS Map 120; ref SK 471707

Bolsover Castle

Eyam Moor Tumulus and Stone Circle

This monument is on private land; we regret
that there is currently no public access.
Map 119; ref SK 225790

Hardwick Old Hall

9¹/2m SE of Chesterfield, off A617
Ruins of large house built by Bess of
Hardwick, Countess of Shrewsbury, from
*c.*1587. It had innovative planning, and
still retains interesting decorative
plasterwork. It was superseded by the
adjacent Hardwick Hall, begun in 1590.
Open: Exterior only, open daily until
dusk. Visitors should use National Trust car
park, Easter Saturday–31st October
10.30am–6.30pm. (NT)
OS Map 120; ref SK 463638

Hob Hurst's House

On private land; no public access at present.
OS Map 119; ref SK 287692

Nine Ladies Stone Circle, Stanton Moor

*From unclassified road off A6, 5m SE of
Bakewell*
Stone circle, probably dating from the
early Bronze Age. May have surrounded a
small burial mound.
Open: Any reasonable time.
OS Map 119; ref SK 253635

Peveril Castle

*On S side of Castleton, 15m W of
Sheffield on A625*
12th-century keep and other remains
dramatically sited on a spur high above
the town, giving magnificent views of the
Peak District.
Open: All year. 85p/65p/40p.
Tel: (0433) 20613
OS Map 110; ref SK 150827

Peveril Castle

Sutton Scarsdale Hall

*Between Chesterfield and Bolsover, 1¹/2m
S of Arkwright Town*
Dramatic shell of a great classical
mansion designed by Francis Smith of
Warwick in 1721.
Open: Any reasonable time (exterior
only).
Facilities: **P** &
OS Map 120; ref SK 441690

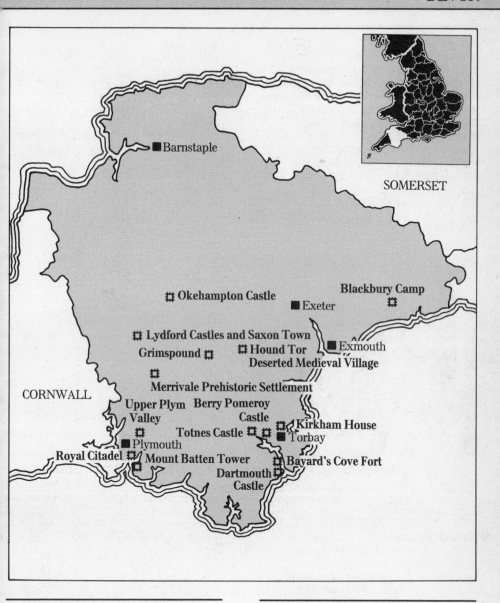

SOMERSET

■ Barnstaple

✠ Okehampton Castle

Blackbury Camp
✠

■ Exeter

✠ Lydford Castles and Saxon Town

Grimspound ✠   ✠ Hound Tor
Deserted Medieval Village

■ Exmouth

✠
Merrivale Prehistoric Settlement

CORNWALL

Upper Plym   Berry Pomeroy
Valley   Castle
✠   Totnes Castle ✠ ✠   ✠ Kirkham House
■ Plymouth   ■ Torbay
Royal Citadel ✠ ✠ Mount Batten Tower   ✠ Bayard's Cove Fort
Dartmouth
Castle

Bayard's Cove Fort, Dartmouth
In Dartmouth, on riverfront
Small artillery fort built 1509–10,
to cover the entrance to the inner
haven.
Open: Any reasonable time.
OS Map 202; ref SX 879510

Blackbury Camp
1½m SW of Southleigh off B3174/A3052
Iron Age hill fort occupied *c.*200BC–
AD100, defended by a bank and ditch,
with a complicated entrance.
Open: Any reasonable time.
OS Map 192; ref SY 188924

● Berry Pomeroy Castle

2½m E of Totnes off A385

Dramatically sited ruins of a large late medieval fortified house, remodelled and ambitiously extended by Protector Somerset in the manner of a French courtier's château, but left unfinished on his execution in 1551.

Open: Summer season. 85p/65p/40p.
Facilities: 🅿 ☕ Toilets ♿(grounds and ground floor only)
Tel: (0272) 734472
OS Map 202; ref SX 839623

Berry Pomeroy Castle

● Dartmouth Castle

1m SE of Dartmouth off B3205 (narrow approach road)

Begun in 1481 and extended in the 16th century, this was one of the earliest castles to be built for artillery and guards the narrow entrance to the Dart estuary. 19th-century coastal defence battery with fully equipped guns.

Open: All year. £1.15/85p/60p.
Facilities: Toilets 🅿 (limited) ☕ ⊗
Tel: (08043) 3588
OS Map 202; ref SX 887503

Grimspound

6m SW of Moretonhampstead off B3212

Late Bronze Age settlement (1000–800BC), consisting of 24 huts within a dry-stone walled area of about 4 acres.

Open: Any reasonable time.
OS Map 191; ref SX 701809

Hound Tor Deserted Medieval Village, Manaton

1½m S of Manaton off Ashburton road. Park in Hound Tor car park, ½m walk

Inhabited from the late Saxon period to *c.*1300, with long-houses for the villagers and their cattle, and buildings with provision for drying corn.

Open: Any reasonable time.
OS Map 191; ref SX 746788

Dartmouth Castle

Kirkham House, Paignton
In Kirkham St, off Cecil Rd, Paignton
Well-preserved 15th-century stone house, probably the home of a prosperous merchant or an official of the Bishop's Palace. Exhibition of modern furniture.
Open: Summer season.
85p/65p/40p.
Facilities: ♿ (ground floor only)
Tel: (0803) 522775
OS Map 202; ref SX 885610

Kirkham House, Paignton

Lydford Castles and Saxon Town
In Lydford off A386 8m S of Okehampton
Late 12th-century tower used as a prison, with a rectangular bailey to the west lying within the area of a fortified town. The first castle was a late 11th-century military work on the earlier town ramparts.
Open: Any reasonable time.
OS Map 191; Castle ref SX 510848, Fort ref SX 509847

Merrivale Prehistoric Settlement
1m E of Merrivale
Early Bronze Age village with hut circles, two stone rows, three cairns and a burial cist.
Open: Any reasonable time.
OS Map 191; ref SX 553746

Mount Batten Tower
In Plymstock, on Mount Batten Point
30ft high gun-tower built in 1665, with original windows and vaulted roof.
Open: 1st Thur in month 2–4pm, by prior written permission of the Officer Commanding, RAF Mount Batten, Plymouth.
OS Map 201; ref SX 488533

Okehampton Castle
1m SW of Okehampton off A30
Founded in the 11th century, the remains of a Norman keep and motte with 14th-century hall, chapel lodgings and gatehouse in the north bailey. Dismantled after 1538. Picnic area, woodland walks.
Open: All year. 85p/65p/40p.
Facilities: Toilets 🅿 🎧
Tel: (0837) 52844
OS Map 191; ref SX 584942

Okehampton Castle

Royal Citadel, Plymouth
At E end of Plymouth Hoe
One of the large fortifications erected
after the Restoration of the monarchy
in 1660. The elaborate entrance gateway
is dated 1670. Inside is a statue of
George II in classical armour.
Open: Any reasonable time (exterior
only).
OS Map 201; ref SX 480538

● **Totnes Castle**
*In Totnes, on the hill overlooking
the town*
Norman motte-and-bailey castle with
a stone shell-keep and curtain built in
the early 13th century and reconstructed
in the 14th.
Open: All year. 85p/65p/40p.
Facilities: ₽ (70yds, small charge)
Tel: (0803) 864406
OS Map 202; ref SX 800605

Upper Plym Valley
4m E of Yelverton
6 square miles of ancient landscape
preserving evidence of human settlement
and industrial activity from Neolithic
times to the 20th century.
Open: Any reasonable time.
OS Map 202

Totnes Castle

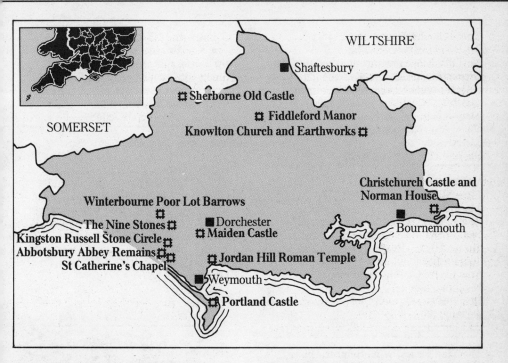

Abbotsbury Abbey Remains
In Abbotsbury, off B3157, near churchyard
The eastern gable of one of the conventual
buildings of Abbotsbury Abbey.
Open: Any reasonable time.
Facilities: 🅿
OS Map 194; ref SY 578852

Christchurch Castle and Norman House
In Christchurch, near the Priory
Early 12th-century Norman keep, and
Constable's House built *c*.1160.
Open: Any reasonable time.
OS Map 195; ref SZ 160927

Fiddleford Manor
1m E of Sturminster Newton off A357
Part of a 14th-century house, altered in the
early 16th century, comprising a hall and
solar block, both with elaborate roofs.
Open: Summer season. 85p/65p/40p.
Facilities: 🅿 ♿ (Ground floor only - 1 step)
Tel: (0258) 72597
OS Map 194; ref ST 801136

Jordan Hill Roman Temple, Weymouth
2m NE of Weymouth off A353
Foundations of small Romano-Celtic temple.
Open: Any reasonable time.
OS Map 194; ref SY 698821

Kingston Russell Stone Circle
2m N of Abbotsbury
A prehistoric circle of 18 stones.
Open: Any reasonable time.
OS Map 194; ref SY 577878

Fiddleford Manor

Knowlton Church and Earthworks
3m SW of Cranborne on B3078
Neolithic henge monument, consisting of a circular ditch with a bank on the outside probably originally containing a timber circle, but now containing a ruined church of Norman origin.
Open: Any reasonable time.
Facilities: &
OS Map 195; ref SU 024100

Maiden Castle
2½m SW of Dorchester off A354
The finest example of a prehistoric fortress in this country, with enormous earthworks and complicated entrances. Stormed by the Roman army during the Conquest in about AD43, it dates from the Iron Age and superseded a Neolithic camp.
Open: Any reasonable time.
Facilities: P
OS Map 194; ref SY 670885

The Nine Stones, Winterbourne Abbas
½m W of Winterbourne Abbas S of A35
Remains of a prehistoric stone circle consisting of nine standing stones.
Open: Any reasonable time.
OS Map 194; ref SY 611904

● Portland Castle
Overlooking Portland harbour adjacent to RN helicopter base
Coastal fort erected by Henry VIII, extended in the 17th century. Changed hands several times in the Civil War, eventually yielding to Parliament in 1646. Small site exhibition.
Open: Summer season. 85p/65p/40p.
Facilities: P ⊗ & (exterior & ground floor only – 1 deep step)
Tel: (0305) 820539
OS Map 194; ref SY 684743

St Catherine's Chapel, Abbotsbury
½m S of Abbotsbury by pedestrian track from village off B3157
Small 15th-century chapel with stone vault and turret used as a lighthouse.
Open: Any reasonable time.
OS Map 194; ref SY 572848

● Sherborne Old Castle
½m E of Sherborne on N side of lake
Built by Roger, Bishop of Salisbury, 1107–1135. The main buildings and curtain wall with towers and gates are of this period. Passed to Sir Walter Raleigh in 1592, but abandoned after the Civil War.
Open: All year. 85p/65p/40p.
Facilities: P ⊗ &
Tel: (093581) 2730
OS Map 183; ref ST 647167

Sherborne Old Castle

Winterbourne Poor Lot Barrows
2m W of Winterbourne Abbas, S of junction of A35 with minor road to Compton Valence
A fine group of Bowl, Bell and Disc barrows of the Bronze Age.
Open: Any reasonable time.
OS Map 194; ref SY 590906

Portland Castle

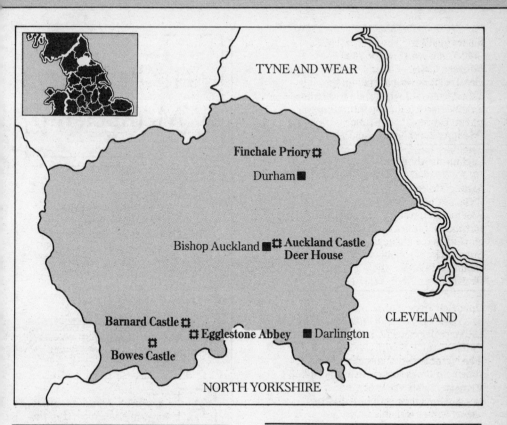

Auckland Castle Deer House, Bishop Auckland
In Bishop Auckland Park, just N of town centre on A689
Deer-shelter in the park of the bishops of Durham, built in 1760 by Bishop Trevor.
Open: Park opening hours.
OS Map 93; ref NZ 216305

Barnard Castle
In Barnard Castle
Extensive castle on the precipitous bank of the River Tees. Remains include parts of 14th-century great hall and a cylindrical 12th-century tower, built by the Baliol family.
Open: All year. 85p/65p/40p.
Facilities: &
Tel: (0833) 38212
OS Map 92; ref NZ 049165

Barnard Castle

Bowes Castle
¼m W of Bowes on A66, 4m W of Barnard Castle
Massive stone keep three storeys high, dating from *c.*1170, and set within the earthworks of a Roman fort.
Open: Any reasonable time.
OS Map 92; ref NY 992135

Egglestone Abbey
1m S of Barnard Castle on minor road off B6277
Picturesque remains of a Premonstratensian abbey, including a substantial part of the church and remains of the abbey buildings.
Open: Any reasonable time.
Facilities: 🅿 ♿
OS Map 92; ref NZ 062151

● Finchale Priory
3m NE of Durham, on minor road off A167
13th-century Benedictine priory erected on the site of St Godric's hermitage. Considerable remains of church and abbey buildings survive in a peaceful setting by the River Wear.
Open: All year. 85p/65p/40p (free during winter season).
Facilities: 🅿 ♿
Tel: (091) 386 3828
OS Map 88; ref NZ 297471

Finchale Priory

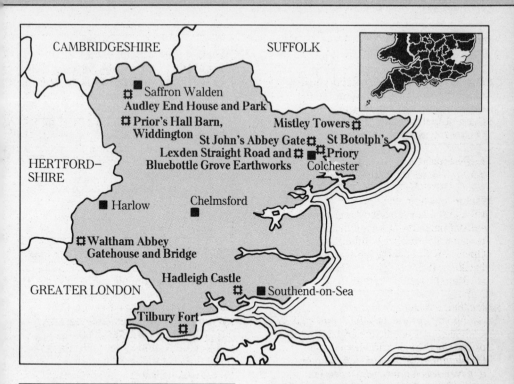

- **Audley End House and Park**
- *1m W of Saffron Walden on B1383*
- *(M11 exits 8, 9 Northbound only, & 10)*

Palatial Jacobean house, remodelled in the 18th and early 19th centuries. Magnificent plaster ceilings, reception rooms by Robert Adam, 'Strawberry Hill gothick' chapel and some splendidly atmospheric 19th-century interiors. The house is authentically displayed with original furniture and pictures. 'Capability' Brown landscape park with garden buildings by Adam.
Open: Summer season, Tues-Sun, 1-6pm; park and gardens open at 12 noon. Last admissions one hour before closing. Closed Mondays except Bank Holidays. £3.50/£2.60/£1.75.
Facilities: Toilets ✕ 🅿 ♫ Souvenir shop ♿ (substantial ground-floor area & gardens only)
Tel: (0799) 22399
OS Map 154; ref TL 525382

Colchester: Lexden Straight Road and Bluebottle Grove Earthworks
2m W of Colchester off A604
Parts of the series of earthworks protecting pre-Roman Colchester which probably date to the 1st century AD, and consisting of one single and one triple bank-and-ditch.
Open: Any reasonable time.
OS Map 168; ref TL 963240

Audley End House

Hadleigh Castle
¾m S of A13 at Hadleigh
Castle founded in 1231, but largely
reconstructed in the 14th century. It
had a large courtyard with stone
curtain wall and towers, of which two
survive almost to their full height.
Open: Any reasonable time.
Facilities: & (hilly)
Te: (0702) 555 632
OS Map 178; ref TQ 810860

Mistley Towers
On B1352, 1½m E of A137 at Lawford,
9m E of Colchester
Two towers designed by Robert Adam and
built in 1776, which originally stood
at either end of a church demolished in
the 19th century.
Open: Any reasonable time. Keykeeper.
Facilities: & (exterior only)
OS Map 169; ref TM 116320

● Prior's Hall Barn, Widdington
In Widdington, on unclassified road 2m
SE of Newport (off B1383)
One of the finest surviving medieval
barns in south-east England and
representative of the group of aisled
barns centred on north-west Essex.
Open: Summer season, weekends and Bank
Holidays only 10am–6pm. 60p/45p/30p.
Facilities: &
Tel: (0799) 41047
OS Map 167; ref TL 538319

Prior's Hall Barn, Widdington

St Botolph's Priory, Colchester
Colchester, near St Botolph's station
Nave of 11th- or early 12th-century church
of the first Augustinian priory in England.
Open: Any reasonable time.
OS Map 168; ref TL 999249

St John's Abbey Gate, Colchester
On S side of central Colchester
Fine 15th-century abbey gatehouse in
East Anglian flintwork.
Open: Any reasonable time (exterior
only).
Facilities: &
OS Map 168; ref TL 998248

● Tilbury Fort
½m E of Tilbury off A126
The outstanding example in England of 17th-
century military engineering, with later
alterations showing the development of
fortifications over the next 200 years.
Open: All year. £1.15/85p/60p.
Facilities: Education room. Toilets 🅿 ☕
& (exterior, fort square & magazines)
Tel: (0375) 858489
OS Map 177; ref TQ 651754

Tilbury Fort

Waltham Abbey Gatehouse and Bridge
In Waltham Abbey off A112
Late 14th-century abbey gatehouse and
part of the north cloister range, with
Harold's Bridge, probably 14th-century.
Open: Any reasonable time.
OS Map 166; ref TL 381008

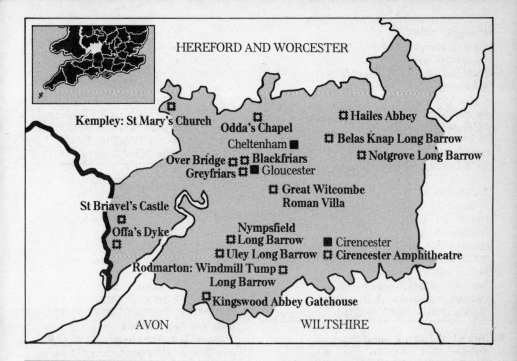

HEREFORD AND WORCESTER

Kempley: St Mary's Church
Odda's Chapel
Hailes Abbey
Cheltenham ■
Belas Knap Long Barrow
Notgrove Long Barrow
Over Bridge ✚✚ Blackfriars
Greyfriars ✚■ Gloucester
Great Witcombe
Roman Villa
St Briavel's Castle
Offa's Dyke
Nympsfield
Long Barrow
Cirencester ■
Uley Long Barrow
Cirencester Amphitheatre
Rodmarton: Windmill Tump ✚
Long Barrow
Kingswood Abbey Gatehouse
AVON
WILTSHIRE

Belas Knap Long Barrow
2m S of Winchcombe, near Charlton Abbots
Fine example of a Neolithic long barrow,
with a false portal at the north end. The
earthen mound is surrounded by a dry-built
stone revetting wall, with four burial
chambers entered from the sides.
Open: Any reasonable time.
OS Map 163; ref SP 021254

Gloucester, Blackfriars
*In Ladybellegate St off Southgate St
and Blackfriars Walk*
Dominican house founded in 1239.
Surviving remains include the friary
church and parts of the cloister and its
surrounding buildings.
Open: Exterior viewing only. Interior
access by appointment only: tel (0272)
734472.
OS Map 162; ref SO 830186

Cirencester Amphitheatre
*Next to bypass on W of town – park
in town or on Cotswold Ave to S of
Amphitheatre by obelisk*
Roman Amphitheatre dating from the 2nd
century, possibly fortified in the 5th
century. One of the largest and best
preserved in Britain.
Open: Any reasonable time.
OS Map 163; ref SP 020014

Gloucester, Blackfriars

Gloucester, Greyfriars
On Greyfriars Walk, behind Eastgate
Market off Southgate St
Remains of late 15th-/early 16th-century
Franciscan friary church.
Open: Any reasonable time.
Facilities: &
OS Map 162; ref SO 830186

Great Witcombe Roman Villa
5m SE of Gloucester, off A417, 1/2m S of
reservoir in Witcombe Park
Large villa built round three sides of
a courtyard.
Open: Any reasonable time.
Facilities: P &
OS Map 163; ref SO 899144

● Hailes Abbey
2m NE of Winchcombe off A46
Cistercian abbey founded in 1246; ruins
of the monastic buildings and
cloister. Site museum contains a fine
collection of architectural fragments
and tiles.
Open: All year. £1.15/85p/60p. (NT)
Facilities: Toilets P ♫
& (general access, 1 step to museum)
Tel: (0242) 602398
OS Map 150; ref SP 050300

Hailes Abbey

Kempley: St Mary's Church
1m N of Kempley off B4024, 6m NE of
Ross-on-Wye
11th-century church containing superb
wall paintings dating from 12th, 13th
and 14th centuries.
Open: Any reasonable time. Keykeeper.
For details of where key may be obtained
tel. Area Office: (0272) 734472.
OS Map 149; ref SO 672296

Kingswood Abbey Gatehouse
In Kingswood off B4060 1m SW of
Wotton-under-Edge
Late 14th-century gatehouse, all that
remains of the Cistercian abbey founded
by William de Berkeley in 1139.
Open: Any reasonable time (exterior
only)
Facilities: & (exterior only)
OS Map 162; ref ST 748919

Notgrove Long Barrow
1 1/2m NW of Notgrove off B4068
Neolithic burial mound with chambers
for human remains opening from a
stone-built central passage.
Open: Any reasonable time.
Facilities: P
OS Map 163; ref SP 096211

Nympsfield Long Barrow
1m NW of Nympsfield on B4066
Chambered long barrow dating from the
Neolithic period.
Open: Any reasonable time.
Facilities: P
OS Map 162; ref SO 795014

Odda's Chapel, Deerhurst
In Deerhurst (off B4213) at Abbots
Court SW of parish church
Pre-Conquest chapel founded by Earl
Odda and dedicated in 1056. The nave
survives virtually to its full height
and is divided from the chancel by an
arch.
Open: Any reasonable time.
OS Map 150; ref SO 869298

Offa's Dyke
½m SE of Tintern (access suitable only for those wearing proper walking shoes; not suitable for the young, old or infirm)
Section of the great earthwork built by Offa, King of Mercia 757–96 to mark the boundary of his kingdom.
Open: Any reasonable time.
OS Map 162; ref SO 545005

Over Bridge
1m NW of Gloucester city centre at junction of A40 (Ross) & A419 (Ledbury)
A single span bridge over the River Severn built by Telford 1825–30.
Open: Any reasonable time.
OS Map 162; ref SO 817196

Rodmarton: Windmill Tump Long Barrow
1m SW of Rodmarton off A433 6m SW of Cirencester
Chambered long barrow dating from the Neolithic period.
Open: Any reasonable time.
OS Map 163; ref ST 933973

St Briavel's Castle
7m NNE of Chepstow off B4228
12th-century castle, adjacent to a fine Norman church.
Open: Any reasonable time (exterior only).
OS Map 162; ref SO 559046

Uley Long Barrow (Hetty Pegler's Tump)
3½m NE of Dursley on B4066
Neolithic burial mound of earth about 180ft long, surrounded by a dry-built revetting wall and containing a central passage of stone with three burial chambers.
Open: Any reasonable time.
OS Map 162; ref SO 790000

Opening times

All year

Good Friday or 1 April*–30 Sept:
Open daily 10am–6pm

1 Oct–Maundy Thursday or 31 March*:
Open daily 10am–4pm;
closed Mondays, 24–26 Dec, 1 Jan

Summer season

Good Friday or 1 April*–30 Sept:
Open daily 10am–6pm.

*whichever is earlier

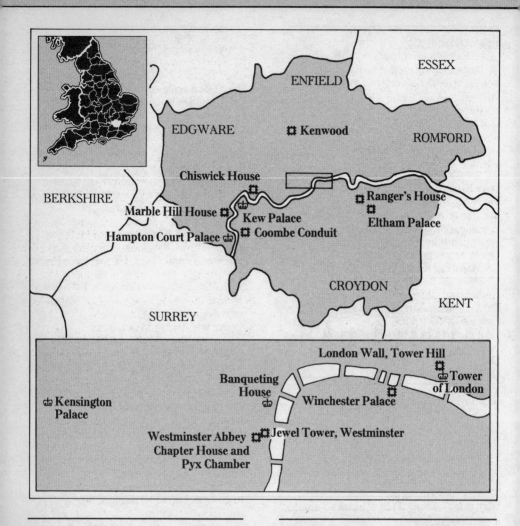

ESSEX

ENFIELD

EDGWARE

🏛 Kenwood

ROMFORD

Chiswick House

Ranger's House 🏛

BERKSHIRE

Marble Hill House 🏛

Kew Palace

Eltham Palace

Hampton Court Palace ♛

Coombe Conduit

CROYDON

KENT

SURREY

London Wall, Tower Hill

Banqueting
House

🏛 Tower
of London

♛ Kensington
Palace

Winchester Palace

Westminster Abbey 🏛 Jewel Tower, Westminster
Chapter House and
Pyx Chamber

● **Banqueting House** (Historic Royal Palaces)
Whitehall, opposite Horse Guards, SW1
Designed by Inigo Jones for James I and
built 1619–22 as part of the old Palace
of Whitehall, with a magnificent
ceiling painted by Rubens. Scene of King
Charles I's execution in 1649.
Open: Tues-Sat 10am–5pm, Sun
2–5pm. Closed Good Friday, 24–26
Dec, 1st January & Mondays & at short
notice for government functions.
Facilities: audio tour
Tel: 01-930 4179 (071)

Banqueting House, Whitehall

● **Chiswick House**
Burlington Lane, W4
Palladian villa designed by the third
Earl of Burlington *c.*1725 with interior
decoration by William Kent. Kent also
landscaped the gardens which are
ornamented with classical buildings and
statuary. Some original paintings. New
exhibition on ground floor with film telling
the story of house and grounds.
Open: All year, plus Mondays in winter,
26 Dec & 1 Jan. £1.70/£1.30/85p
(includes free audio tour).
Facilities: Toilets (in grds) ▣ (off west-bound
A4)▰ ♫ ♿ (exterior & ground floor only)
Tel: 01-995 0508 (081)

Chiswick House

● **Coombe Conduit**
Coombe, Kingston-upon-Thames
Finest surviving 16th-century conduit house
built to supply water to Hampton Court
Palace.
Open: Fridays by prior arrangement
with Kingston-upon-Thames Museum and
Heritage Centre.
Tel: 01-546 5386 (081)

● **Eltham Palace**
¾m N of A20 off Court Yard, SE9
Royal manor dating from the 13th
century, largely rebuilt from the 15th
century onwards. Surviving buildings
include the bridge over the moat and
the late 15th-century great hall with
its splendid hammer-beam roof.
Open: Thur & Sun open 11am–4pm
Nov–Mar; 11am–7pm Apr–Oct. Works to
the Palace will be carried out early
1990. Contact the Army Education
Corps: 01-854 2242 ext 4232. (081)
Facilities: ♿

● **Hampton Court Palace**
(Historic Royal Palaces)
*N of Thames by Hampton Court Bridge,
East Molesey, Surrey KT8 9AU*
The original Tudor Mansion of Hampton
Court was begun in 1514 by Cardinal
Wolsey, who presented it to Henry VIII in
a vain attempt to remain in his favour.
Henry VIII enlarged the building to make it
one of the most splendid Palaces in the
kingdom. Later alterations were made to
update the Palace by Sir Christopher Wren
for William and Mary.
Attractions include: the Gatehouse, the
Astronomical Clock, the Great Hall, the
Chapel Royal, the Tudor Kitchens and Cellars,
the Real Tennis Court, the State and Private
Apartments, the Mantegna Cartoons, the
Renaissance Picture Gallery, the Banqueting
House, the Great Vine, the famous Maze as
well as the magnificent gardens.
Open: mid Mar–mid Oct, daily
9.30am–6pm; mid Oct–mid Mar, daily
9.30am–4.30pm. Last admission ½ hour
before closing. Closed 23–26 December &
1 Jan. Real Tennis Court and Banqueting
House open mid Mar–mid Oct only. *English
Heritage members should note that their
membership allows free admission to the
Palace only, not to the other facilities at
Hampton Court.*
Tel: 01-977 8441 (081)
Facilities: Toilets ✕ ▣
♿ (State Apartments first floor accessible
to groups of up to 10 disabled people).

Hampton Court Palace

● **Jewel Tower, Westminster**
Opposite S end of Houses of Parliament
(Victoria Tower)
Built *c.*1365 for King Edward III
and formerly part of the Palace of
Westminster. Used to house valuables which
formed part of the king's 'wardrobe', and
subsequently used as a storehouse and
government office.
Open: All year. 60p/45p/30p. Liable
to be closed at short notice.
Facilities: &
Tel: 01-222 2219 (071)

● **Kensington Palace** (Historic Royal Palaces)
W side of Kensington Gardens, W8
Nobleman's house converted into a royal
palace by Christopher Wren, with
interior decoration by William Kent and
Grinling Gibbons. Queen Victoria lived here
until she acceded to the throne in 1837.
Although the Palace is still a royal residence,
the State Apartments are open to the public
together with the Court Dress Collection.
Open: Mon–Sat 9am–5pm,
Sun 1–5pm. Last admissions 4.15pm.
Closed Good Friday, 24–26 Dec, 1 Jan.
Tel: 01-937 9561 (071)
Facilities: Toilets & (State Apartments 31
shallow stairs in 3 flights, assistance
available; Court Dress Collection 3 small
steps plus 2 steps in middle of the collection;
toilets for disabled).

Kenwood, The Iveagh Bequest
Hampstead Lane, NW3
Outstanding neo-classical house remodelled
by Robert Adam, 1764–73, who created the
fine Library. The house contains paintings
from the Iveagh Bequest, including works
by Rembrandt, Vermeer, Hals,
Gainsborough, Reynolds and Turner as well
as appropriate Adam furniture. The flower
gardens, woodland and sloping lawns of
Kenwood make an ideal setting for the
concerts, held by the Lake in the summer.
Open: All year, plus Mondays in winter,
26 Dec & 1 Jan.
Facilities: Souvenir shop, toilets ▣ ✕ ♫
&(no steps; toilets for disabled)
Tel: 01-348 1286 (081)

Kenwood

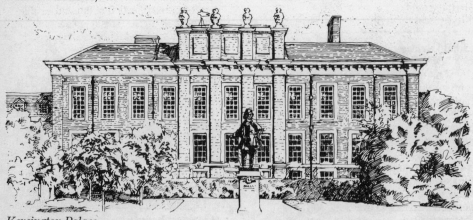

Kensington Palace

Kew Palace (Historic Royal Palaces)
Royal Botanic Gardens,
Richmond-upon-Thames
17th-century merchant's house, known as
the Dutch House, which was bought by
George III in 1781 and occupied as a
royal residence until 1818. Queen
Charlotte's Cottage, built about 1772,
which is also in the gardens (about a mile
away), is also open to the public.
Open: April–Sept, Palace daily 11am–
5.30pm, Queen's Cottage weekends & Bank
Holidays 11am–5.30pm.
Tel: 01-940 3321 (081)
Facilities: Toilets (inside Botanical
Gardens) ▣

Kew Palace

London Wall, Tower Hill
Near Tower Hill underground station, EC3
Part of the eastern defences of the
City of London, founded on Roman work
of about AD200, heightened in the
Middle Ages.
Open: Any reasonable time.
Facilities: Toilets ♿

Marble Hill House
Richmond Road, Twickenham
Complete example of an English Palladian
villa built 1724–29, with grounds going
down to the Thames, and now containing an
important collection of early Georgian
paintings and furniture, including a unique
set of architectural paintings by Panini.
Open: All year, plus Mondays in winter,
26 Dec & 1 Jan.
Facilities: Toilets ✖ ♫ ▣ (at Richmond end of
Marble Hill park) ♿(exterior & ground floor
only; toilets for disabled)
Tel: 01-892 5115 (081)

Marble Hill House

Ranger's House
Chesterfield Walk, Blackheath, SE10
The home of the 4th Earl of Chesterfield,
a handsome red brick villa built *c.*1700.
Houses a remarkable series of Jacobean
portraits and a collection of musical
instruments.
Open: All year, plus Mondays in winter,
26 Dec & 1 Jan.
Facilities: Toilets ▣ (in Chesterfield Walk;
limited) ♿ (lift for disabled; toilets for
disabled)
Tel: 01-853 0035 (081)

Ranger's House

● **Tower of London** (Historic Royal Palaces)
N of Thames by Tower Bridge, E1
Royal fortress founded in the
11th century and since then a focal
point in English history. Today a
centre of pageantry and ceremonial,
home of the Crown Jewels and of the
finest collection of armour in Britain.
Open: Mar–Oct Mon–Sat 9.30am–
5pm, Sun 2–5pm; Nov–Feb Mon–Sat
9.30am–4pm. Closed Good Friday,
24–26 Dec, 1 Jan & Sundays from Nov–Feb.
Jewel House closed February. *Members must
collect free ticket from main shop prior to entry.*
Tel: 01-709 0765 (071)
Facilities: Toilets 🍵
♿ (grounds, Oriental, History &
Ordnance Galleries, upper floor of Jewel
House. Many areas are cobbled. Toilets
for disabled)

Tower of London

● **Westminster Abbey Chapter House,
Pyx Chamber and Abbey Museum**
*Approach either through the Abbey or
through Dean's Yard and the cloister*
The Chapter House was built by the
royal masons *c.*1250 and contains two of
the finest examples of medieval English
sculpture, a contemporary tiled floor and
a series of mural paintings. The 11th-
century Pyx Chamber now houses the
Abbey treasures. The Abbey Museum
contains medieval royal effigies.
Open: All year, plus Mondays in winter.
Liable to be closed at short notice on state
occasions. £1.60/80p/40p.
Facilities: Souvenir shop 🎧
Tel: 01-222 5897 (071)

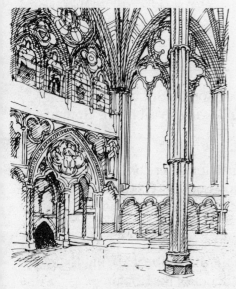

Westminster Abbey Chapter House

Winchester Palace, Southwark
*Near Southwark Cathedral, at corner of
Clink St & Storey St, SE1*
Part of the 13th-century great hall of
the town house of the Bishops of
Winchester, destroyed by fire in 1814.
Open: Any reasonable time.
Facilities: Toilets ♿

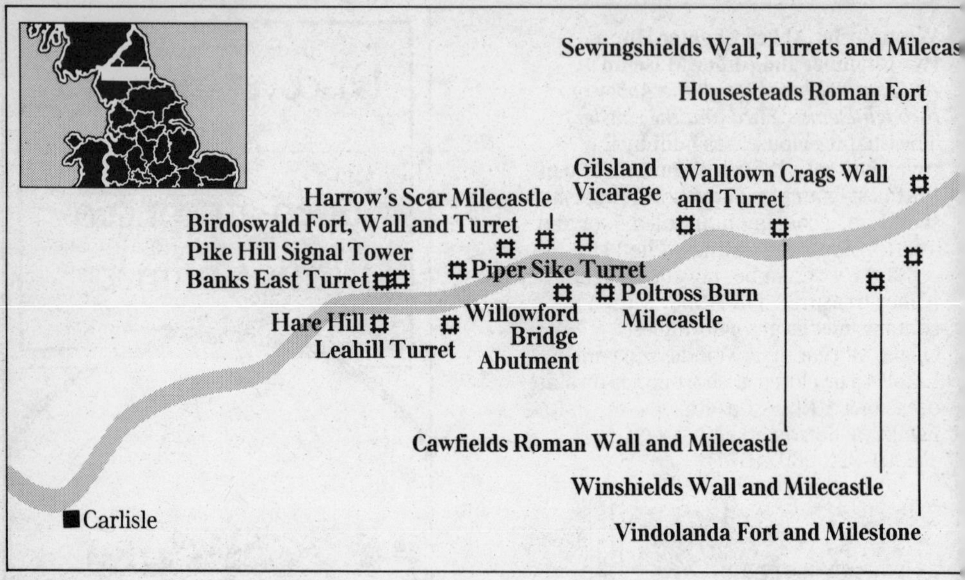

Sewingshields Wall, Turrets and Milecas

Housesteads Roman Fort

Gilsland Vicarage Walltown Crags Wall and Turret

Harrow's Scar Milecastle

Birdoswald Fort, Wall and Turret

Pike Hill Signal Tower

Banks East Turret Piper Sike Turret

Hare Hill Willowford Bridge Abutment

Leahill Turret

Poltross Burn Milecastle

Cawfields Roman Wall and Milecastle

Winshields Wall and Milecastle

Carlisle

Vindolanda Fort and Milestone

Hadrian's Wall – the northern frontier of Roman Britain – was constructed between AD122 and 125, following a visit by the Roman Emperor Hadrian to Britain in AD122.

Along its length of 80 Roman miles, small forts were built every mile (milecastles) and, between them, look-out towers (turrets). The wall was later modified when larger forts were added at about seven-mile intervals.

The wall was finally abandoned late in the 4th century AD, but today remains as a fine monument to the splendour of the Roman Empire's past.

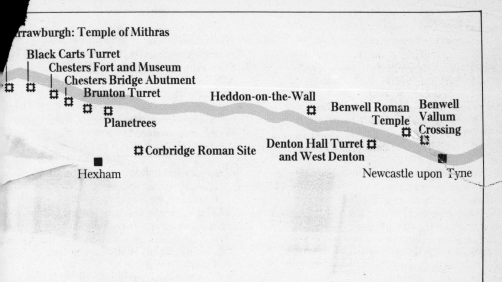

Arrawburgh: Temple of Mithras
Black Carts Turret
Chesters Fort and Museum
Chesters Bridge Abutment
Brunton Turret
Heddon-on-the-Wall
Benwell Roman Temple
Benwell Vallum Crossing
Planetrees
Denton Hall Turret and West Denton
Corbridge Roman Site
Hexham
Newcastle upon Tyne

Banks East Turret (52a)
On minor road E of Banks village,
3½m NE of Brampton
Well-preserved 'Turf Wall' turret, with
characteristic plinth at front and back.
Open: Any reasonable time.
Facilities: 🅿
OS Map 86; ref NY 575647

Benwell Roman Temple
Immediately S of A69 at Benwell in
Broomridge Ave
Small temple dedicated to the local god
Antenociticus with the apse at its
south end, containing a statue base and
flanked by altars.
Open: Any reasonable time.
OS Map 88; ref NZ 217646

Benwell Vallum Crossing
Immediately S of A69 at Benwell in
Denhill Park Ave
An original causeway across the Vallum
ditch giving access to Condercum fort
to the north.
Open: Any reasonable time.
OS Map 88; ref NZ 215646

Birdoswald Fort, Wall and Turret
2¾m W of Greenhead, on minor road
off B6318
5-acre fort for cohort of 1000 men on
the site of a 'Turf Wall' turret. East
and south gateways are well-preserved;
angle and interval turrets visible.
Open: Any reasonable time. (The site is in
the care of Cumbria County Council who
levy a charge for admission; reduced for
EH members.)
OS Map 86; ref NY 615663

Black Carts Turret (29a)
2m W of Chollerford on B6318
Turret with 500-yd length of wall and ditch.
Open: Any reasonable time.
OS Map 87; ref NY 884712

Brunton Turret (26b)
¼m S of Low Brunton on A6079
One of the best-preserved turrets on
the line of the wall, with a 70-yd
stretch of wall.
Open: Any reasonable time.
Facilities: 🅿 on nearby A6079.
OS Map 87; ref NY 922698

Carrawburgh: Temple of Mithras
3¾m W of Chollerford on B6318
The worship of Mithras, a sun-god, was popular with the Roman army. The 3rd-century 'mithraeum' outside the fort was the latest and largest of such buildings to occupy the site.
Open: Any reasonable time.
Facilities: ▣
OS Map 87; ref NY 869713

Cawfields Roman Wall and Milecastle (42)
1¼m N of Haltwhistle off B6318
Well preserved milecastle at the west end of almost ¾ mile of wall.
Open: Any reasonable time.
Facilities: Toilets ▣
OS Map 87; ref NY 716667

Chesters Bridge Abutment
On E bank of North Tyne opposite Chesters Fort, on footpath from B6318 (½m,
Remains of the Roman bridge which carried Hadrian's Wall across the North Tyne river, east of the fort at Chesters. Parts of at least two successive Roman bridges can be seen.
Open: Any reasonable time.
OS Map 87; ref NY 914700

● Chesters Fort and Museum (Cilurnum)
½m W of Chollerford on B6318
A 6-acre fort for 500 cavalrymen. Remains include gateways, commandant's house, headquarters building and a fine example of a bath house. The museum houses a collection of sculptures and Roman inscriptions.
Open: All year, plus Mondays in winter. £1.40/£1.05/70p.
Facilities: Souvenir shop, toilets ▣ ♿ ⅃
Tel: (0434) 681379
OS Map 87; ref NY 913701

Chesters Fort

● Corbridge Roman Site (Corstopitum)
½m NW of Corbridge on minor road
Site on the main road from York to Scotland, occupied in succession by a series of forts, a military depot and a town. The museum records this history and displays finds from the site.
Open: All year. £1.40/£1.05/70p.
Facilities: Souvenir shop, toilets ▣ ⅃
Tel: (0434) 632349
OS Map 87; ref NY 983649

Denton Hall Turret (7b) and West Denton
4m W of Newcastle city centre on A69
Turret and section of wall 70yd to the west. The turret retains the base of the platform on which rested the ladder to the upper floor.
Open: Any reasonable time.
OS Map 88; ref NZ 195656

Gilsland Vicarage Roman Wall
In former vicarage garden, Gilsland village
220yd of wall, showing narrow wall on broad foundation.
Open: Any reasonable time.
OS Map 86; ref NY 632662

Hare Hill
¾m NE of Lanercost, off minor road
Short length of wall standing 9ft high.
Open: Any reasonable time.
OS Map 86; ref NY 562646

Harrow's Scar Milecastle (49)
¼m E of Birdoswald Fort, 2¾m W of Greenhead, on minor road off B6318
Remains of stone milecastle, preceded by one of turf, linked to Birdoswald Fort by an impressive length of wall.
Open: Any reasonable time.
OS Map 86; ref NY 621664

Corbridge Roman Site

Heddon-on-the-Wall
Immediately E of Heddon village, S of A69
Fine stretch of 280yd of wall. The circular chamber near the west end is a medieval kiln.
Open: Any reasonable time.
OS Map 88; ref NZ 136669

● Housesteads Roman Fort (Vercovicium)
2¾m NE of Bardon Mill on B6318
A 5-acre fort for 1000 infantry, with extensive civil settlement to the south. Walls, gateways, headquarters, granaries and other buildings including the latrine can be seen. The small museum contains altars, inscriptions and models. Striking views of the surrounding landscape.
Open: All year, plus Mondays in winter.
£1.40/£1.05/70p. (NT)
Facilities: Toilets 🅿 (both on main road, ½m to S) ♥ ♿ (car park at site; enquire at NT/National Park information centre on main road)
Tel: (0434) 344363
OS Map 87; ref NY 790687

Housesteads Roman Fort

Leahill Turret (51b)
On minor road 2m W of Birdoswald Fort
'Turf Wall' turret. The space between turret and ditch is typical of 'Turf Wall' structures.
Open: Any reasonable time.
OS Map 86; ref NY 585653

Pike Hill Signal Tower
On minor road E of Banks village
The remains of a Roman signal tower 20ft square, placed at angle of 45° to the wall.
Open: Any reasonable time.
Facilities: 🅿
OS Map 86; ref NY 577648

Vindolanda Fort

Piper Sike Turret (51a)
On minor road 2m W of Birdoswald Fort
'Turf Wall' turret, built before the
Stone Wall which abuts against the
turret's east and west walls.
Open: Any reasonable time.
OS Map 86; ref NY 588654

Planetrees Roman Wall
1m SE of Chollerford on B6318
50-ft length of narrow wall on broad
foundation, showing extensive
rebuilding in Roman times.
Open: Any reasonable time.
OS Map 87; ref NY 928696

Poltross Burn Milecastle (48)
*Immediately SW of Gilsland village,
by old railway station*
One of the best-preserved milecastles
on the wall, with remains of north and
south gates, enclosing walls and a pair
of small barrack blocks.
Open: Any reasonable time.
Facilities: P near Station Hotel
OS Map 86; ref NY 634662

Sewingshields Wall, Turrets and Milecastle (35)
*In the vicinity of T34a, N of minor
road, 1½m E of Housesteads Fort*
Two Roman miles of wall, largely
unexcavated but preserving traces of a
milecastle and turrets. Vallum, Military Way
and ditch are well preserved for the eastern
700yd next to the road.
Open: Any reasonable time.
OS Map 87; ref NY 813702

● Vindolanda Fort and Roman Milestone
*1¼m SE of Twice Brewed, on minor
road off B6318*
3½-acre fort south of the wall in which
3rd-century buildings and walls replaced
earlier structures of wood and stone. A
milestone stands by the road, the Stanegate,
which passes the north gate.
Open: All year. (Access controlled by
the Vindolanda Trust; English Heritage
members are admitted to site at half-price.
Full price is payable if members visit the
museum)
Facilities: Toilets P ☕ (Vindolanda Trust)
Tel: (04984) 277
OS Map 87; ref NY 771664

Walltown Crags Wall and Turret (45a)
1m NE of Greenhead off B6318
400yd of wall and a turret predating
the wall about 100yd short of the
normal turret position, possibly
because it formed part of some
long-distance signalling system.
Open: Any reasonable time.
Facilities: P nearby
OS Map 87; ref NY 674664

Willowford Bridge Abutment
W of minor road ¾m W of Gilsland
1000yd of wall, including two turrets,
ending at the bridge abutment, much
altered in Roman times owing to changes
in the course of the river and consequent
rebuilding of the bridge.
Open: Any reasonable time. (Access
controlled by Willowford Farm; small charge
levied)
OS Map 86; ref NY 629664

Winshields Wall and Milecastle (40)
*W of Steel Rigg car park, on minor
road off B6318*
350yd of wall, with unexcavated milecastle
at its eastern end. This fine stretch of wall,
7ft 6in thick as elsewhere on the crags,
includes the highest point on the wall.
Open: Any reasonable time.
OS Map 87; ref NY 745676

BERKSHIRE

⚏ Silchester Roman City Wall

■ Basingstoke

SURREY

WILTSHIRE

⚏ Flowerdown Barrows

⚏ The Grange, Northington

Wolvesey ⚏ ■ Winchester

Medieval Merchant's House ⚏

⚏ Bishop's Waltham Palace

WEST SUSSEX

Southampton ■ ⚏ Netley Abbey

Titchfield Abbey ⚏

Portchester Castle ⚏

DORSET

Calshot Castle ⚏ ⚏ Portsmouth

Fort Brockhurst ⚏

King James's and Landport Gates ⚏

Garrison Church

⚏ Hurst Castle

ISLE OF WIGHT

● Bishop's Waltham Palace

In Bishop's Waltham

Extensive ruins of a fortified palace of the Bishops of Winchester, founded in the 12th century and consisting of buildings dating mainly from the 12th and 14th centuries ranged round a courtyard and enclosed within a moat. Ground floor of Dower House furnished as 19th-century farmhouse with exhibition upstairs.

Open: All year. £1.15/85p/60p.
Facilities: Toilets (opposite car park on other side of main road) 🅿 ♿ (grounds only)
Tel: (0489) 892460
OS Map 185; ref SU 552173

Bishop's Waltham Palace

Calshot Castle
On spit 2m SW of Fawley off B3053
Coastal fort completed in 1540 as part of
Henry VIII's chain of coastal defences.
Exhibition and recreated pre-World War I
barrack room.
Open: Summer season. £1.15/85p/60p.
Facilities: ▣ Toilets
Tel: (0703) 892023
OS Map 196; ref SU 488025

Calshot Castle

Flowerdown Barrows
*In Littleton, 2½m NW of Winchester
off A272*
Round barrows, once part of a larger group.
Open: Any reasonable time.
OS Map 185; ref SU 459320

Fort Brockhurst
*Off A32, in Gunner's Way, Elson,
on N side of Gosport*
One of five major forts built in the
mid 19th century to protect the Gosport
peninsula and Portsmouth naval base.
Exhibition illustrates the history of
Portsmouth's defences.
Open: All year. £1.15/85p/60p.
Facilities: Education room available
all year round. Toilets ▣
& (grounds & ground floor only)
Tel: (0705) 581059
OS Map 196; ref SU 596020

The Grange, Northington
4m N of New Alresford off B3046
One of the most important neo-classical
country houses in Europe, built *c.*1809
in the form of a Greek temple round the
core of a late 17th-century brick
mansion. Site exhibition.
Open: Any reasonable time (exterior
viewing only).
Facilities: ▣ & (with assistance)
OS Map 185; ref SU 562362

Hurst Castle
*On Pebble Spit S of Keyhaven. Best
approached by ferry from Keyhaven*
Coastal fort erected by Henry VIII with
extensive 19th- and 20th-century
additions. Site exhibition.
Open: Summer season, daily;
winter, weekends only, 10am–4pm.
£1.15/85p/60p.
Facilities: Toilets ✕
Tel: (05904) 2344
OS Map 196; ref SZ 319898

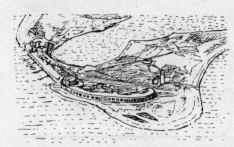

Hurst Castle

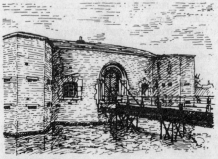

Fort Brockhurst

Netley Abbey
In Netley, 7m SE of Southampton,
facing Southampton Water
Extensive remains of Cistercian abbey
founded in 1239, including the walls of
the church and cloister buildings, converted
in Tudor times for use as a house,
now ruined.
Open: Summer season, daily; winter,
weekends only, 10am–4pm. 85p/65p/40p.
Facilities: 🅿 &
Tel: (0703) 453076
OS Map 196; ref SU 453089

Netley Abbey

● Portchester Castle
On S side of Portchester off A27
Medieval castle with an almost perfect
Norman keep and an Augustinian priory
church within the walls and bastions of
a large late Roman fort. Exhibition opening
spring 1990 covers 1400 years of history
and features artefacts from the castle.
Open: All year. £1.15/85p/60p.
Facilities: 🅿 Toilets in Car Park 🐾 ⊗
& (grounds & lower levels only)
Tel: (0705) 378291
OS Map 196; ref SU 625046

● Portsmouth: Garrison Church
On Grand Parade S of Portsmouth High St
Originally a 13th-century
hospital, converted into a chapel in
the 16th century, which was restored by
the Victorian architect G E Street.
Open: Summer season. 60p/45p/30p.
Facilities: 🅿 &
Tel: (0705) 823973
OS Map 196; ref SU 633992

Garrison Church

Portsmouth: King James's and Landport Gates
King James's Gate: forms entrance to
United Services Recreation Ground
(officers) on Park Rd; Landport Gate:
as above, men's entrance on St George's Rd
Gates of the defences of Portsmouth,
refurbished from 1665 by Charles II.
The former was completed in 1687,
the latter in 1698.
Open: Any reasonable time (exteriors
only).
OS Map 196; King James's Gate ref
SU 638000, Landport Gate ref SU 634998

Portchester Castle

Silchester Roman City Wall
1m E of Silchester
The almost complete circuit of the
early 3rd-century town walls of the
tribal capital of Calleva Atrebatum.
Open: Any reasonable time.
OS Map 175; ref SU 643624

● **Southampton: Medieval Merchant's
House**
*58 French Street, ¼m S of city centre just off
Castle Way (between High St and Bugle St)*
Restored and furnished late 13th-century
merchant's house. Shop sells wine, beer,
herbs and spices, pottery etc.
Open: All year. £1.40/£1.05/70p (includes
free audio tour). Free admission to shop.
Facilities: Toilets ♫ ♿ (ground floor only
via side door)
Tel: (0703) 221503
OS Map 196; ref SU 419112

Medieval Merchant's House

● **Titchfield Abbey**
½m N of Titchfield off A27
Originally a Premonstratensian abbey
founded in 1232 and dissolved in 1537,
converted into a mansion by the Earl of
Southampton, with nave of the monastic
church partly preserved in the later building.
Open: Summer season.
85p/65p/40p.
Facilities: 🅿 ♿
Tel: (0329) 43016
OS Map 196; ref SU 541067

● **Wolvesey: Old Bishop's Palace**
*¼m SE of Winchester Cathedral, next to
the Bishop's Palace; access from College St*
Ruins of extensive medieval palace of the
Bishops of Winchester, built round a
quadrangular courtyard.
Open: Summer season.
85p/65p/40p.
Facilities: ♿
Tel: (0962) 54766
OS Map 185; ref SU 484291

Wolvesey: Old Bishop's Palace

Titchfield Abbey

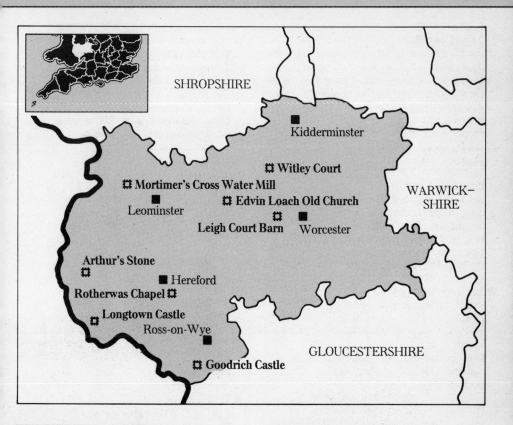

SHROPSHIRE

Kidderminster

✜ Witley Court

✜ Mortimer's Cross Water Mill

✜ Edvin Loach Old Church

Leominster

Leigh Court Barn   Worcester

WARWICK–SHIRE

Arthur's Stone
✜

■ Hereford

Rotherwas Chapel ✜

✜ Longtown Castle

Ross-on-Wye

GLOUCESTERSHIRE

✜ Goodrich Castle

Arthur's Stone, Dorstone
7m E of Hay-on-Wye off B4348 near Dorstone
Prehistoric burial chamber and entrance passage formed by large blocks of stone.
Open: Any reasonable time.
OS Map 148; ref SO 319431

● ### Goodrich Castle
5m S of Ross-on-Wye off A40
Superbly sited castle, hewn from the red sandstone on which it stands above the River Wye. Extensive remains mainly date from the 13th and 14th centuries, but incorporate a 12th-century keep.
Open: All year. £1.15/85p/60p.
Facilities: Toilets ₽
Tel: (0600) 890538
OS Map 162; ref SO 579199

Edvin Loach Old Church
4m N of Bromyard on unclassified road off B4203
Remains of early Romanesque church.
Open: Any reasonable time.
Facilities: ₽
OS Map 149; ref SO 663585

Goodrich Castle

Leigh Court Barn
*5m W of Worcester on unclassified road
off A4103*
Magnificent timber-framed barn, built in the
early 14th-century for the monks of Pershore
Abbey. It is the largest cruck-built structure
in Britain.
Open: Summer season: Thur, Fri,
Sat & Sun 10am–6pm.
OS Map 150; ref 784534

Longtown Castle
4m WSW of Abbey Dore
Small Marcher castle below the Black
Mountains. Motte with fine cylindrical
keep of *c.*1200 and walled inner bailey.
Open: Any reasonable time.
OS Map 161; ref SO 321291

● Mortimer's Cross Water Mill
7m NW of Leominster on B4362
Built in the 18th century and still in
use in the 1940's, the mill is still in
working order.
Open: 1 Apr–30 Sept: Thur, Sun
and Bank Holidays only 2–6pm.
60p/45p/30p.
Facilities: & (exterior & ground floor only)
OS Map 148; ref SO 426637

Mortimer's Cross Water Mill

● Rotherwas Chapel
1½m SE of Hereford on B4399
14th-century chapel largely rebuilt in
the 1580s for the Roman Catholic
Bodenham family, restored and extended
by EW Pugin in 1868.
Open: Summer season, 10am–6pm,
weekends only. 60p/45p/30p.
Facilities: ▣ & (kissing gate)
OS Map 149; ref SO 537383

Rotherwas Chapel

● Witley Court
10m NW of Worcester on A443
Spectacular ruins of a country house on
a huge scale, once the home of the Earls
of Dudley. Cast in its present form by the
architect Samuel Daukes in the 1860s,
incorporating earlier porticoes by Nash.
Open: Summer season. 60p/45p/30p.
Facilities: ▣
OS Map 150; ref 769649

Witley Court

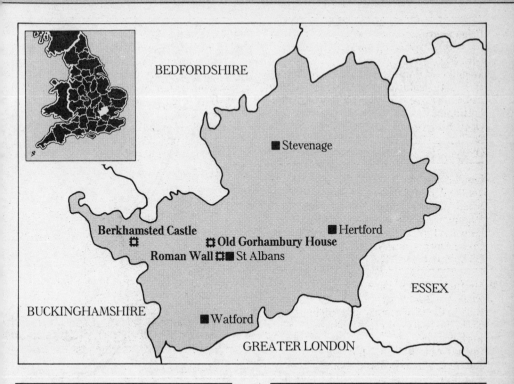

Berkhamsted Castle
Adjacent to Berkhamsted station
Extensive remains of a large
11th-century motte-and-bailey castle,
with remains of curtain wall and
towers, and possibly a chapel.
Open: Any reasonable time.
Tel: (0442) 862411
OS Map 165; ref SP 996083

Old Gorhambury House
*¼m W of Gorhambury House & accessible
only through private drive from A4147 at
St Albans (2m)*
Surviving remains of a mansion built by
Sir Nicholas Bacon in 1563–68. The
porch of the great hall shows the impact
of the Renaissance on English building.
Open: May–Sept, Thurs only 2–5pm,
or at other times by appointment.
Tel: (0727) 54051 (mornings only).
OS Map 166; ref TL 110077

St Albans: Roman Wall
*On S side of St Albans, ½m from centre
off A4147*
Several hundred yards of the wall built about
AD200, which enclosed the Roman city of
Verulamium. It had projecting towers at
intervals and was backed by an earthen
rampart. Foundations survive of one of
the gateways.
Open: Any reasonable time.
OS Map 166; ref TL 135067

**For full details of
opening times see page 4**

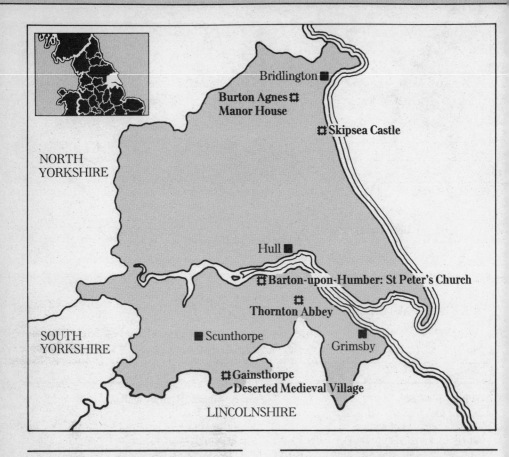

Barton-upon-Humber: St Peter's Church
In Barton-upon-Humber
10th-century church with later nave and
chancel, formerly Barton parish church.
Exhibition on history of the church.
Open: Mon–Fri 2–4pm. Weekends
by appointment only – tel. Area Office:
(0904) 658626.
OS Map 112; ref TA 034220

Burton Agnes Manor House
*Burton Agnes village, 5m SW of
Bridlington on A166*
A rare example of a Norman house,
altered and encased in brick in the
17th and 18th centuries.
Open: All year.
OS Map 101; ref TA 103633

Gainsthorpe Deserted Medieval Village
*On minor road W of A15 S of
Hibaldstow 5m SW of Brigg
(no directional signs)*
Earthworks of the peasant houses,
gardens and streets of deserted
medieval village.
Open: Any reasonable time.
OS Map 112; ref SK 955012

Skipsea Castle
8m S of Bridlington, W of Skipsea village
A Norman motte-and-bailey castle. The
outer bailey is in the care of English
Heritage.
Open: Any reasonable time.
OS Map 107; ref TA 163551

Thornton Abbey
10m NE of Scunthorpe on minor road N of A160
Augustinian abbey founded in 1139. Magnificent 14th-century gatehouse and ruins of the abbey church, octagonal chapter house and other buildings. Small exhibition of finds from the site in the gatehouse.
Open: Summer season, daily, but gatehouse and sales office may be closed some days; telephone before your visit to avoid disappointment. Winter, weekends only 10am–4pm. 85p/65p/40p.
Facilities: P ♿ (except interior of gatehouse and part of chapter house ruins)
Tel: (0469) 40357
OS Map 113; ref TA 115190

Thornton Abbey

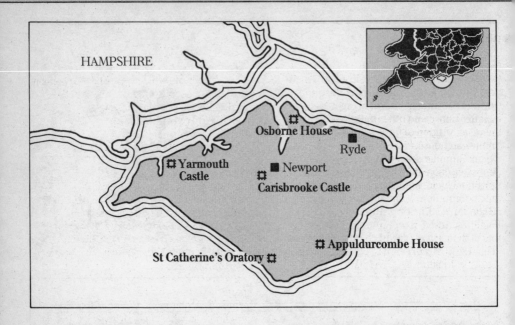

HAMPSHIRE

Osborne House

Ryde

Yarmouth
Castle

Newport

Carisbrooke Castle

Appuldurcombe House

St Catherine's Oratory

● **Appuldurcombe House**
½m W of Wroxall off B3327
Shell of a grand house begun in 1701
and standing in a fine park landscaped
by 'Capability' Brown.
Open: All year. 85p/65p/40p.
Facilities: Toilets 🅿 ▱
♿ (¼m walk uphill from car park)
Tel: (0983) 852484
OS Map 196; ref SZ 543800

● **Carisbrooke Castle**
1¼m SW of Newport
Splendid castle, dating from Norman
times and best known as the prison of
Charles I in 1647–48. The Governor's
Lodge houses the island's County Museum.
Open: All year, plus Mondays in winter.
£2.30/£1.70/£1.15.
Facilities: Toilets 🅿 ✕ (April–Sept) ♫
♿ (grounds & lower levels only)
Tel (0983) 522107
OS Map 196; ref SZ 486877

Appuldurcombe House

Carisbrooke Castle

Osborne House

1m SE of East Cowes

Queen Victoria's seaside home, built at her own expense in 1845, and designed under the supervision of the Prince Consort by Thomas Cubitt. The Queen died at Osborne in 1901 and her private apartments have been preserved largely unaltered since then.

Open: Summer season, house 10am–5pm (last admission 4.30pm), grounds 10am–6pm; 1–31 Oct, house and grounds open daily 10am–5pm (last admission 4pm). £3.20/£2.40/£1.60.

Facilities: Souvenir shop, education room, toilets 🅿 ✕ ♿ (exterior & ground floor only: vehicles with disabled passengers may set them down at house entrance before returning to car park)

Tel: (0983) 200022

OS Map 196; ref SZ 516948

Osborne House

St Catherine's Oratory

¾m NW of Niton

West tower of the 14th-century chapel of St Catherine, which was used as a beacon or lighthouse following the wreck of the wine ship 'St Marie' of Bayonne.

Open: Any reasonable time.

Facilities: 🅿

OS Map 196; ref SZ 494773

Yarmouth Castle

In Yarmouth adjacent to car ferry terminal

Last of the coastal defence forts built by Henry VIII, completed in 1547. Has the earliest surviving angle bastion in England. In the 17th century the moat was filled in and the castle reduced in size. Site display and exhibition of paintings.

Open: Summer season. £1.15/85p/60p.

Facilities: ♿ (ground floor only)

Tel: (0983) 760678

OS Map 196; ref SZ 354898

Yarmouth Castle

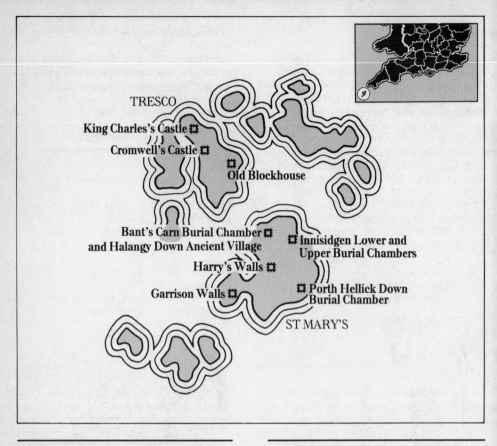

TRESCO

King Charles's Castle ✿
Cromwell's Castle ✿
✿ Old Blockhouse

Bant's Carn Burial Chamber ✿
and Halangy Down Ancient Village
✿ Innisidgen Lower and
Upper Burial Chambers
Harry's Walls ✿
Garrison Walls ✿
✿ Porth Hellick Down
Burial Chamber
ST MARY'S

St Mary's: Bant's Carn Burial Chamber and Halangy Down Ancient Village
1m N of Hugh Town
Bronze Age burial mound with entrance passage and chamber. Nearby are remains of an Iron Age village, still used in Roman times.
Open: Any reasonable time.
OS Map 203; ref SV 911124

St Mary's: Garrison Walls
Around the headland W of Hugh Town
Fortified walls encircling the headland west of Hugh Town, begun about 1600 and added to in 1715–46 as part of the island's defences. Small site exhibition.
Open: Any reasonable time.
OS Map 203; ref SV 898104

St Mary's: Harry's Walls
¼m NE of Hugh Town
Uncompleted 16th-century fort intended to command the harbour of St Mary's Pool.
Open: Any reasonable time.
OS Map 203; ref SV 910110

St Mary's: Innisidgen Lower and Upper Burial Chambers
1¾m NE of Hugh Town
Two Bronze Age cairns, both containing burial chambers, about 100 metres apart.
Open: Any reasonable time.
OS Map 203; ref SV 921127

St Mary's: Porth Hellick Down Burial Chamber
1½m E of Hugh Town
Probably the best-preserved Bronze Age burial mound on the Islands, with entrance passage and chamber.
Open: Any reasonable time.
OS Map 203; ref SV 929108

Tresco: Cromwell's Castle
200yd W of King Charles's Castle, ¾m NW of New Grimsby
17th-century round tower built to command the haven of New Grimsby, begun after the Civil War and altered in the 18th century.
Open: Any reasonable time.
OS Map 203; ref SV 882159

Tresco: King Charles's Castle
¾m NW of New Grimsby
Castle built during the reign of Edward VI (1547–53) for coastal defence, with 17th-century additions.
Open: Any reasonable time.
OS Map 203; ref SV 882161

Tresco: Old Blockhouse
On Blockhouse Point, at S end of Old Grimsby harbour
Gun tower built in the mid-16th century.
Open: Any reasonable time.
OS Map 203; ref SV 898155

Lessons to Remember

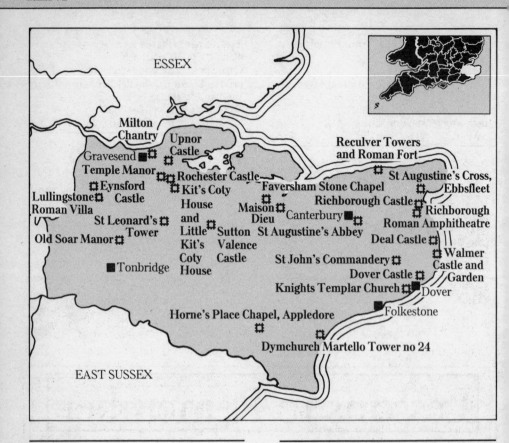

ESSEX

Milton Chantry
Upnor Castle
Gravesend
Reculver Towers and Roman Fort
Temple Manor
Rochester Castle
St Augustine's Cross
Eynsford Castle
Kit's Coty House and Little Kit's Coty House
Faversham Stone Chapel
Ebbsfleet
Lullingstone Roman Villa
Richborough Castle
Maison Dieu
Canterbury
Richborough Roman Amphitheatre
St Leonard's Tower
Old Soar Manor
Sutton Valence Castle
St Augustine's Abbey
Deal Castle
Tonbridge
St John's Commandery
Walmer Castle and Garden
Dover Castle
Knights Templar Church
Dover
Horne's Place Chapel, Appledore
Folkestone
Dymchurch Martello Tower no 24

EAST SUSSEX

● **Deal Castle**
SW of Deal town centre
Largest and most complete of the coastal forts built by Henry VIII in answer to the fear of invasion by the Catholic powers of Europe. Exhibition on Henry VIII's coastal defences.
Open: All year. £1.15/85p/60p.
Facilities: Souvenir shop, toilets 🍽️🎧
& (courtyards & ground floor only)
Tel: (0304) 372762
OS Map 179; ref TR 378521

For full details of opening times see page 4

Deal Castle

Dover Castle

● Dover Castle
On E side of Dover
One of the largest and strongest castles in
Britain, dominating the shortest passage
from the Continent. The curtain walls
enclose a Roman lighthouse, a Saxon church,
a fine Norman keep and underground works.
Special attractions include All the Queens
Men exhibition and Battle of Waterloo model.
Open: All year, plus Mondays in winter.
£3.00/£2.00/£1.50.
Facilities: Shop, toilets ☐ ✕ (for
private functions tel. 0304 205830),
🎧 (underground works), education room
♿ (courtyards & grounds – some very
steep slopes)
Tel: (0304) 201628
OS Map 179; ref TR 326416

Dover: Knights Templar Church
On the Western Heights above Dover
Foundations of a small circular
12th-century church.
Open: Any reasonable time.
OS Map 179; ref TR 313408

Dymchurch Martello Tower no 24
Access from High Street, not from seafront
One of 74 towers built along the coast
between 1805 and 1812 to resist the
threatened French invasion.
Open: Summer season.
85p/65p/40p.
Tel: (0303) 873684
OS Map 189; ref TR 102294

Dymchurch Martello Tower no 24

Eynsford Castle
In Eynsford off A225
Small 11th-century castle preserving
the greater part of its high curtain
wall and a stone hall.
Open: All year.
Facilities: ▣ &
Tel: (0322) 862536
OS Map 177; ref TQ 542658

Faversham Stone Chapel
1¼m W of Faversham on A2
Remains of small medieval church
incorporating part of a 4th-century
Romano-British pagan mausoleum.
Open: Any reasonable time.
OS Map 178; ref TQ 992614

Horne's Place Chapel, Appledore
1½m N of Appledore
14th-century domestic chapel with
undercroft, once attached to the manor
house.
Open: Wed only, 10am–5pm.
Facilities: ▣
OS Map 189; ref TQ 957307

Kit's Coty House and Little Kit's Coty House
W of A229 2m N of Maidstone
Ruins of two prehistoric burial chambers,
formerly covered by long earthen mounds.
Open: Any reasonable time.
OS Map 188; ref TQ 745608 & 745604

Lullingstone Roman Villa
½m SE of Eynsford off A225
Large country villa, occupied through
much of the Roman period and revealing
four distinct periods of building.
Splendid mosaics in the reception rooms.
Open: All year. £1.15/85p/60p (includes
free audio tour).
Facilities: Toilets ▣ ♫
OS Map 177; ref TQ 529651

Lullingstone Roman Villa

Milton Chantry, Gravesend
E of central Gravesend off A226
14th-century building which housed the
chapel of a leper hospital and the chantry
of the de Valence and Montechais families.
Changing exhibition of local arts and crafts.
Open: Summer season. 60p/45p/30p.
Tel: (0474) 321520
OS Map 177; ref TQ 652743

Milton Chantry

Old Soar Manor, Plaxtol
1m E of Plaxtol
Fine example of a late 13th-century knight's
residence, with solar (over a vaulted
undercroft) and chapel. Exhibition.
Open: Summer season. (NT)
Facilities: ▣ (limited)
Tel: (0732) 810622
OS Map 188; ref TQ 619541

Ospringe: Maison Dieu
In Ospringe on A2 ½m W of Faversham
Early 16th-century timber-framed
building incorporating fragments of a
13th-century hospital and shelter for
pilgrims. Site museum.
Open: Summer season, weekends only
10am–6pm. 85p/65p/40p.
Facilities: Toilet
Tel: (0795) 533751
OS Map 178; ref TR 002608

Maison Dieu

Reculver Towers and Roman Fort
At Reculver 3m E of Herne Bay
Remains of Saxon and Norman church, of
which the 12th-century towers are a
famous landmark, within the walls of a
Roman fort.
Open: Summer season. 85p/65p/40p.
Facilities: Toilets ▣ & (ground floor
only–long slope up from car park)
Tel: (02273) 66444
OS Map 179; ref TR 228694

Richborough Castle
1½m N of Sandwich off A257
Seaport where the Romans landed in AD43;
defensive earthworks were replaced in
the 3rd century by the massive stone walls
which still survive. Site museum.
Open: All year. 85p/65p/40p.
Facilities: ▣ & ♫
Tel: (0304) 612013
OS Map 179; ref TR 324602

Richborough Castle

Richborough Roman Amphitheatre
1¼m N of Sandwich off A257
Amphitheatre associated with the nearby
3rd-century castle.
Open: Any reasonable time.
OS Map 179; ref TR 321598

Reculver Towers

● **Rochester Castle**
By Rochester Bridge (A2)
Large 11th-century castle partly
founded on the Roman city wall, with a
splendid keep of *c.*1130.
Open: All year. £1.15/85p/60p.
Facilities: Toilets (public, in castle
grounds), shop. ∩
Tel: (0634) 402276
OS Map 178; ref TQ 742686

Rochester Castle

● **St Augustine's Abbey, Canterbury**
In Longport ¼m E of Cathedral Close
Remains of Benedictine monastery,
including the Norman church with its
well-preserved crypt, on the site of
the abbey founded in 598 by St
Augustine.
Open: All year. 85p/65p/40p.
Facilities: ▣ (nearby)   & (some steps)
Tel: (0227) 767345
OS Map 179; ref TR 154578

St Augustine's Cross, Ebbsfleet
2m E of Minster off B2048
A modern cross marking the traditional
site of St Augustine's landing in 597.
Open: Any reasonable time.
Facilities: &
OS Map 179; ref TR 340641

St Leonard's Tower, West Malling
On unclassified road W of A228
Fine early Norman tower, probably built
*c.*1080 by Gundulf, Bishop of Rochester.
Open: Any reasonable time.
Facilities: & (grounds only)
OS Map 188; ref TQ 675570

Sutton Valence Castle
*5m SE of Maidstone in Sutton Valence
village on A274*
Ruins of 12th-century stone keep positioned
to monitor an important Medieval route
across the Weald from Rye to Maidstone.
Open: Any reasonable time.
OS Map 188; ref TR 815491

Swingfield: St John's Commandery
2m NE of Densole off A260
A medieval chapel built by the Knights
Hospitallers, converted into a farmhouse
in the 16th century and preserving a fine
moulded plaster ceiling and a remarkable
medieval timber roof.
Open: Contact Area Office for details.
OS Map 179; ref TR 232440

St Augustine's Abbey

● Temple Manor, Rochester

In Strood (Rochester) off A228
13th-century great chamber (on a vaulted undercroft) of a manor house of the Knights Templar.
Open: Summer season.
60p/45p/30p.
Facilities: 🅿 ♿ (grounds only)
Tel: (0634) 718743
OS Map 178; ref TQ 733686

Temple Manor

● Upnor Castle

At Upnor, on unclassified road off A228
A fort with a large angle bastion facing the river, built 1560–63 to protect Queen Elizabeth's warships moored in the Medway alongside the new dockyard at Chatham. Exhibition.
Open: Summer season.
85p/65p/40p.
Facilities: Toilets 🅿 (at a slight distance from castle – park before village) ♿ (grounds only)
Tel: (0634) 718742
OS Map 178; ref TQ 758706

Upnor Castle

● Walmer Castle and Garden

On coast S of Walmer
One of the coastal castles built by Henry VIII and the official residence of the Lords Warden of the Cinque Ports, including the Duke of Wellington who died at Walmer and whose furnished rooms have been preserved unaltered.
Open: All year, but closed January and February and when Lord Warden is in residence. £1.70/£1.30/85p.
Facilities: Toilets 🅿 ➥ ♫
♿ (courtyards & gardens only)
Tel: (0304) 364288
OS Map 179; ref TR 378501

Walmer Castle

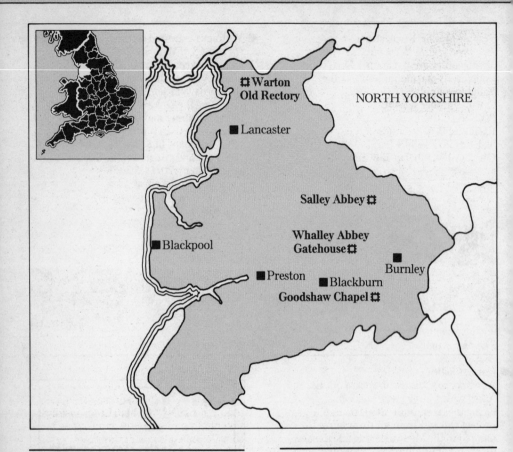

Goodshaw Chapel

2m N of Rawtenstall on minor road E of A682
18th-century Baptist chapel with an almost unaltered set of galleries, pews and pulpit dating from *c*.1800.
Open: Keykeeper. Details at Chapel or tel Area Office: (0904) 658626.
OS Map 103; ref SD 815263

Salley Abbey

At Sawley 3½m N of Clitheroe off A59
Remains of Cistercian abbey founded in 1147.
Open: All year.
Facilities: &
OS Map 103; ref SD 776464

Warton Old Rectory

At Warton, 1m N of Carnforth on minor road off A6
Ruins of a 14th-century rectory with hall, chambers and domestic offices.
Open: All year.
Facilities: &
OS Map 97; ref SD 499723

Whalley Abbey Gatehouse

In Whalley, 6m NE of Blackburn on minor road off A59
Outer gatehouse of the abbey originally with a chapel on the first floor and side chambers flanking the gate passage.
Open: Any reasonable time.
Facilities: &
OS Map 103; ref SD 730360

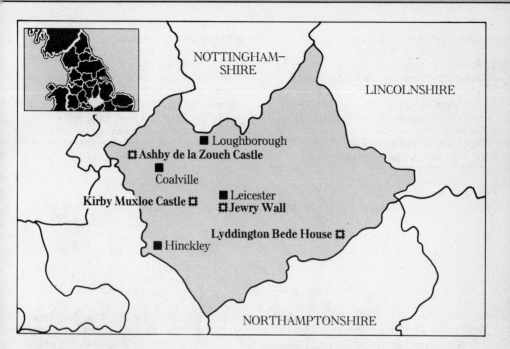

NOTTINGHAM–
SHIRE

LINCOLNSHIRE

■ Loughborough
⌗ **Ashby de la Zouch Castle**
■
Coalville

Kirby Muxloe Castle ⌗

■ Leicester
⌗ Jewry Wall

Lyddington Bede House ⌗

■ Hinckley

NORTHAMPTONSHIRE

● **Ashby de la Zouch Castle**
In Ashby de la Zouch, 12m S of Derby on A50
Remains of a castle built around an earlier manor house by Edward IV's Lord Chamberlain, William Lord Hastings. Dominated by the ruins of a great lodging tower, with spiral staircase and underground tunnel.
Open: All year. 85p/65p/40p.
Facilities: ▣ & (grounds only)
Tel: (0530) 413343
OS Map 128; ref SK 363167

Ashby de la Zouch Castle

● **Kirby Muxloe Castle**
4m W of Leicester off B5380
Moated, brick-built quadrangular castle, begun in 1480 by William Lord Hastings. Potentially a residence of grandeur and considerable strength, it was left unfinished after Hastings was executed in 1483.
Open: All year. 85p/65p/40p.
Facilities: ▣ &
Tel: (0533) 386886
OS Map 140; ref SK 524046

Kirby Muxloe Castle

Leicester: Jewry Wall
In St Nicholas St W of church of St Nicholas
One of the best lengths of Roman wall in the country. Over 30ft high, it formed one side of the exercise hall of the civic baths in the Roman city of Ratae Coritanorum.
Open: Any reasonable time.
OS Map 140; ref SK 583044

● **Lyddington Bede House**
In Lyddington, 6m N of Corby, 1m E of A6003
Only surviving part of a manor house belonging to the Bishops of Lincoln, converted into an almshouse in 1602. The first-floor hall has an elaborate 16th-century timber ceiling.
Open: Summer season. 85p/65p/40p.
Facilities: ♿ (ground-floor rooms only)
Tel: (057282) 2438
OS Map 141; ref SP 875970

Lyddington Bede House

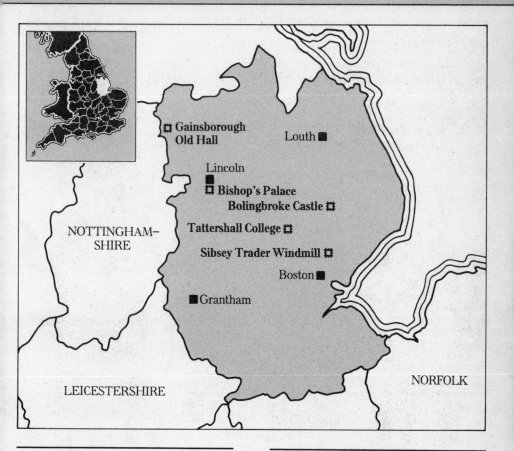

Map showing: Gainsborough Old Hall, Louth, Lincoln, Bishop's Palace, Bolingbroke Castle, Tattershall College, Sibsey Trader Windmill, Boston, Grantham, NOTTINGHAMSHIRE, LEICESTERSHIRE, NORFOLK

Bolingbroke Castle

In Old Bolingbroke, 16m N of Boston off A16
Excavated remains of a hexagonal
castle, probably 13th-century, with
five towers and a gatehouse. Birthplace
of King Henry IV in 1367 and besieged
by Parliamentary forces in 1643.
Open: Any reasonable time.
OS Map 122; ref TF 349649

Gainsborough Old Hall

● Gainsborough Old Hall

In Gainsborough, opposite the Library
One of the largest and most complete late
medieval houses in the country, built by Sir
Thomas de Burgh. Managed by the county
council, it houses a variety
of historical items, furniture and
several exhibitions.
Open: Easter Sat-31 Oct, Mon-Sat 10am-
5pm, Sun 2-5pm; 1 Nov-Maundy Thursday,
Mon–Sat, 10am–5pm. Closed Good Friday,
24–26 Dec. £1.00/50p (includes free audio
tour). No reductions for students/
unemployed.
Facilities: **P** Toilets 🍽 🎧 ♿ (great hall only)
Tel: (0427) 2669
OS Map 121; ref SK 815895

● **Lincoln: Bishop's Palace**
S side of Lincoln cathedral
Ruins of the medieval palace of the
Bishops of Lincoln, including two halls and
a 15th-century gate tower.
Open: Summer season.
60p/45p/30p.
OS Map 121; ref SK 981717

Bishop's Palace

Sibsey Trader Windmill

● **Sibsey Trader Windmill**
*¹/₂m W of village of Sibsey, off A16 5m N
of Boston*
Brick-built tower mill with six sails,
built in 1877, with machinery still intact.
Site exhibition, occasional milling days.
Open: Summer season.
60p/45p/30p.
Facilities: Toilets ℙ
⚹ (exterior & grounds)
Tel: (0205) 750036
OS Map 122; ref TF 345511

Tattershall College
*In Tattershall (off Market Place)
14m NE of Sleaford on A153*
Remains of a grammar school for the
church choristers built in the mid 15th
century by the builder of Tattershall
Castle, Ralph, Lord Cromwell.
Open: Any reasonable time.
OS Map 122; ref TF 213577

Opening times

All year

Good Friday or 1 April* – 30 Sept:
Open daily 10am-6pm

1 Oct-Maundy Thursday or 31 March*:
Open daily 10am-4pm;
closed Mondays, 24-26 Dec, 1 Jan.

Summer season

Good Friday or 1 April* – 30 Sept:
Open daily 10am-6pm.

*whichever is earlier

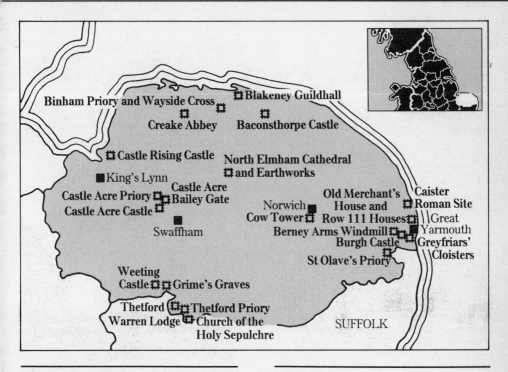

Binham Priory and Wayside Cross

Blakeney Guildhall

Creake Abbey

Baconsthorpe Castle

Castle Rising Castle

North Elmham Cathedral and Earthworks

King's Lynn

Castle Acre Priory

Castle Acre Bailey Gate

Castle Acre Castle

Swaffham

Norwich

Cow Tower

Old Merchant's House and Row 111 Houses

Berney Arms Windmill

Burgh Castle

St Olave's Priory

Caister Roman Site

Great Yarmouth

Greyfriars' Cloisters

Weeting Castle

Grime's Graves

Thetford Warren Lodge

Thetford Priory

Church of the Holy Sepulchre

SUFFOLK

Baconsthorpe Castle

3/4m N of village of Baconsthorpe off unclassified road 3m E of Holt
Large moated and fortified house
built by the Heydon family in the
15th century. The remains include the inner
and outer gatehouse and the curtain wall.
Open: Any reasonable time.
Facilities: **P**
OS Map 133; ref TG 122382

● Berney Arms Windmill

*3 1/2m NE of Reedham on N bank of River
Yare. Accessible by boat, by train to
Berney Arms station (1/4m walk) or by
footpath from Halvergate (3 1/2m).*
One of the best and largest of the
marsh mills remaining in Norfolk. It
has seven floors, making it a landmark
for miles around, and is in working
order. Site exhibition.
Open: Summer season. 85p/65p/40p.
Tel: (0493) 700605
OS Map 134; ref TG 465051

Berney Arms Windmill

Binham Priory
¼m NW of village of Binham on Wells road off B1388
Remains of an early 12th-century Benedictine priory. The nave is intact and used as the parish church, while the rest of the buildings are preserved as ruins.
Open: Any reasonable time.
OS Map 132; ref TF 982399

Binham Wayside Cross
On village green adjacent to Priory
A medieval wayside cross.
Open: Any reasonable time.
OS Map 132; ref TF 982399

Blakeney Guildhall
In Blakeney off A149
Surviving brick-vaulted undercroft (an early example of the use of brick) of a two- or perhaps three-storey 14th-century flint building, probably a merchant's house.
Open: Any reasonable time.
OS Map 133; ref TG 030441

Burgh Castle
At far W end of Breydon Water, on unclassified road 3m W of Great Yarmouth
Rectangular Roman fort walls with projecting bastions, built in the late 3rd century to defend the coast against Saxon raiders.
Open: Any reasonable time.
OS Map 134; ref TG 475046

Caister Roman Site
Near Caister-on-Sea, 3m N of Great Yarmouth
Remains of a Roman site, possibly a fort, revealed by excavation, including part of a defensive wall, a gateway and buildings along a main street.
Open: Any reasonable time.
OS Map 134; ref TG 518125

Castle Acre: Bailey Gate
In Castle Acre, at E end of Stocks Green, 5m N of Swaffham
North gate to the medieval planned town of Acre.
Open: Any reasonable time.
OS Map 132; ref TF 817152

Castle Acre Castle
At E end of Castle Acre 5m N of Swaffham
Remains of Norman house and castle with impressive earthworks.
Open: Any reasonable time.
OS Map 132; ref TF 819152

● Castle Acre Priory
¼m W of village of Castle Acre, 5m N of Swaffham
Extensive remains of Cluniac priory, including the 12th-century church with elaborate west front, and monastic buildings including the prior's lodging and chapel. 15th-century gatehouse. Site exhibition.
Open: All year. £1.15/85p/60p.
Facilities: Shop, toilets ▣ ● ♫ ♿ (ground floor & grounds only)
Tel: (0760) 755394
OS Map 132; ref TF 814148

Castle Acre Priory

Castle Rising Castle
4m NE of King's Lynn off A149
Fine mid 12th-century domestic keep with
a notable history, set in the centre of a
massive earthwork. Other remains include
the bridge and gatehouse to the inner ward.
Open: All year. 85p/65p/40p.
Facilities: Shop, toilets P
& (exterior only; toilets for disabled)
Tel: (055387) 330
OS Map 132; ref TF 666246

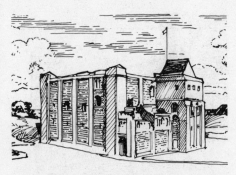

Castle Rising Castle

Creake Abbey
1m N of North Creake off B1355
Ruins of the crossing and eastern arm
of the church of a house of Augustinian
canons founded in 1206.
Open: Any reasonable time.
OS Map 132; ref TF 856395

Great Yarmouth: Old Merchant's House, Row 111 Houses and Greyfriars' Cloisters
Great Yarmouth, ½m inland from beach
Typical 17th-century town houses, one with
splendid plaster ceilings, containing
extensive displays of local architectural and
domestic fittings. Nearby are the remains of
a 13th-century Franciscan friary, including
wall paintings and part of the only vaulted
Franciscan cloister to survive in England.
Open: Summer season.
Entry by tour only. 60p/45p/30p.
Tel: (0493) 857900
OS Map 134; Houses ref TG 525072;
Cloisters ref TG 525073

Grime's Graves
7m NW of Thetford off A134
An extensive group of Neolithic flint
mines, unique in this country, ranging
from shallow pits to deep shafts with
radiating galleries.
Open: All year. 85p/65p/40p.
Facilities: P ♨ & (exhibition area
only; access track rough)
Tel: (0842) 810656
OS Map 144; ref TL 818898

Grime's Graves

Old Merchant's House

North Elmham Cathedral and Earthworks
6m N of East Dereham on B1110
Ruins of a church, possibly the Saxon
cathedral of c.1000, converted into
a manor house by the Bishop of Norwich in
the 14th century and enclosed within
medieval earthworks.
Open: Any reasonable time.
OS Map 132; ref TF 988217

Norwich: Cow Tower
In Norwich, near cathedral
Circular brick tower forming part of
the 14th-century defences of the city.
Open: Any reasonable time.
OS Map 134; ref TG 240091

St Olave's Priory
5¹/₂m SW of Great Yarmouth on A143
Remains of a small Augustinian priory
of c.1216, which includes a
single-aisled church and part of the
cloisters with a fine brick undercroft
in the south range, an exceptionally
early use of this material.
Open: Any reasonable time.
OS Map 134; ref TM 459996

Thetford: Church of the Holy Sepulchre
On W side of Thetford off B1107
Ruined nave of priory church of the Canons
of the Holy Sepulchre, the only standing
remains in England of a house of this order.
Open: Any reasonable time.
OS Map 144; ref TL 865831

● Thetford Priory
On W side of Thetford near station
Extensive ruins of a Cluniac priory
founded in 1103, including the complete
plan of the cloisters and a 14th-
century gatehouse.
Open: Summer season.
85p/65p/40p.
Tel: (0842) 766127
OS Map 144; ref TL 865836

Thetford Priory gatehouse

Thetford Warren Lodge
2m W of Thetford off B1107
Ruins of a small, two-storeyed medieval
house, which probably provided
accommodation for the Priory's gamekeeper.
Open: Any reasonable time.
OS Map 144; ref TL 839841

Weeting Castle
2m N of Brandon off B1106
Ruins of an early medieval manor
house within a rectangular moated
enclosure.
Open: Any reasonable time.
OS Map 144; ref TL 778891

LEICESTERSHIRE

✪ Kirby Hall

Corby ■

Rushton ✪
Triangular Lodge

✪ Geddington:
Eleanor Cross

■
Kettering

Chichele College ✪
Wellingborough ■

Northampton ■

BEDFORDSHIRE

Chichele College
In Higham Ferrers, on A6
Founded by Henry Chichele, Archbishop of Canterbury in 1422 as a college of secular canons. Parts of a quadrangle remain incorporating a chapel.
Open: Any reasonable time (exterior only).
OS Map 153; ref SP 960687

Geddington: Eleanor Cross
In Geddington, off A43 between Kettering and Corby
A cross of elegant design, one of a series erected by Edward I to mark the resting places of the body of his wife Eleanor when brought for burial from Harby in Nottinghamshire to Westminster.
Open: Any reasonable time.
OS Map 141; ref SP 896830

● Kirby Hall

On unclassified road off A43
4m NE of Corby

Outstanding example of a large, stone-built Elizabethan mansion, begun in 1570 with 17th-century alterations. Fine gardens, currently being restored. Site exhibition.
Open: All year. 85p/65p/40p.
Facilities: Toilets ⊡ ☕ 占 (grounds, gardens & ground floor only)
Tel: (0536) 203230
OS Map 141; ref SP 926927

Kirby Hall

● Rushton Triangular Lodge

1m W of Rushton, on unclassified road
3m from Desborough on A6

A unique building, triangular in plan with tripled details symbolising the Holy Trinity, built 1593–97 by Sir Thomas Tresham on his return from imprisonment for his religious beliefs.
Open: Summer season.
85p/65p/40p.
Tel: (0536) 710761
OS Map 141; ref SP 830831

Rushton Triangular Lodge

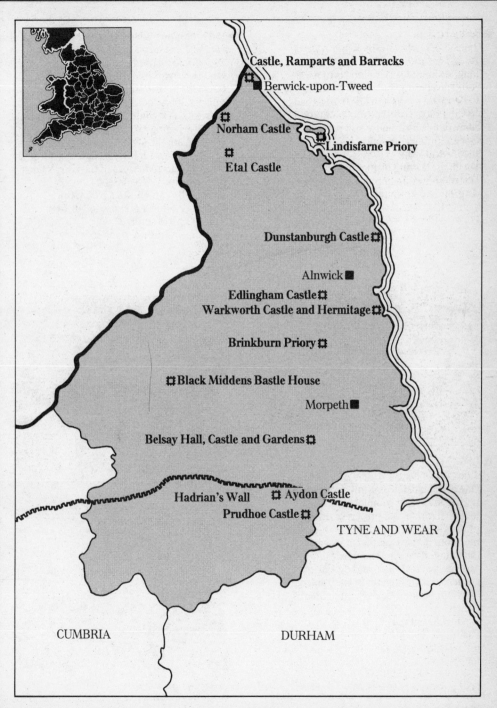

Castle, Ramparts and Barracks

Berwick-upon-Tweed

Norham Castle

Lindisfarne Priory

Etal Castle

Dunstanburgh Castle

Alnwick

Edlingham Castle

Warkworth Castle and Hermitage

Brinkburn Priory

Black Middens Bastle House

Morpeth

Belsay Hall, Castle and Gardens

Hadrian's Wall   Aydon Castle

Prudhoe Castle

TYNE AND WEAR

CUMBRIA

DURHAM

Aydon Castle

1m NE of Corbridge, on minor road off
B6321 or A68

Hall, solar and service blocks of a knight's
residence dating from the late 13th century,
with 'castle' walls and defences added by
1315. Traces of its conversion in the 17th
century to a farmhouse still remain.
Open: Summer season.
£1.15/85p/60p.
Facilities: 'Living history' education
centre, souvenir shop, toilets 🅿 ☕
&. (ground floor only)
Tel: (0434) 632450
OS Map 87; ref NZ 002663

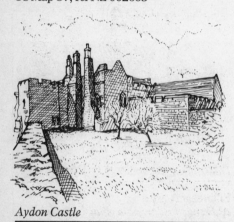

Aydon Castle

Belsay Hall, Castle and Gardens

14m NW of Newcastle on A696

One of the most important neo-classical
houses in Britain completed in 1815,
together with a well preserved 14th-
century castle and a ruined 17th-century
mansion. 30-acre plantsman's garden
including many rhododendrons, heathers,
rare trees and shrubs, and unique quarry
gardens. Exhibition on Belsay; video on
Northumberland Castles; High Sheriff's
Coach.
Open: All year. £1.70/£1.30/85p.
Facilities: Education room, souvenir shop,
toilets ☕ 🅿 &. (grounds only; toilets
for disabled)
Tel: (0661) 881636
OS Map 88; ref NZ 088785

Berwick-upon-Tweed: Berwick Barracks

On the Parade, off Church St,
Berwick town centre

One of the earliest purpose-built
barracks in Britain, built 1717–21 for
officers, men and their families.
Attractions include 'By Beat of Drum', an
award-winning exhibition which recreates
scenes from the life of the English soldier
1660–1880, with life-size figures; Borough
Museum; and Museum of the King's Own
Scottish Border Regiment.
Open: All year. £1.40/£1.05/70p.
Facilities: Souvenir shop, toilets 🅿 ☕
Tel: (0289) 304493
OS Map 75; ref NT 994535

Berwick Barracks

Belsay Hall

Berwick-upon-Tweed Castle

Adjacent to Berwick railway station, W of town centre; accessible also from river bank
West wall of 12th-century castle, with projecting bastions and 16th-century gun tower, which survived as a boundary for the railway yard.
Open: Any reasonable time.
OS Map 75; ref NT 994535

Berwick-upon-Tweed Ramparts

Surrounding Berwick town centre on N bank of River Tweed
Remarkably complete system of fortifications consisting of gateways, ramparts and projecting bastions, built 1558–70 to strengthen or replace the medieval defences begun by Edward I in 1296.
Open: Any reasonable time.
Facilities: ♿ (Toilets & 🅿 in town centre)
OS Map 75; ref NT 994535

Black Middens Bastle House

200yd N of minor road 7m NW of Bellingham; access also along minor road from A68
16th-century stone-built defended farmhouse, with ground-floor accommodation for livestock and living quarters above.
Open: Any reasonable time.
Facilities: 🅿
OS Map 80; ref NY 774900

● Brinkburn Priory

4½m SE of Rothbury off B6334
House of Augustinian canons founded *c*.1135. The late 12th-century church, re-roofed and repaired in 1858, is intact. Beautiful setting by the River Coquet. Short woodland walk from car park.
Open: Summer season.
85p/65p/40p.
Facilities: 🅿
Tel: (066570) 628
OS Map 81; ref NZ 116984

● Dunstanburgh Castle

8m NE of Alnwick, on footpaths from Craster or Embleton
Isolated 14th-century fortress sited on a rocky promontory, high above the sea, which is an important wildlife habitat. Surviving ruins include a substantial gatehouse later converted into a keep, and curtain walls.
Open: All year. 85p/65p/40p. (NT)
Tel: (066576) 231
OS Map 75; ref NU 258220

Dunstanburgh Castle

Edlingham Castle

At E end of Edlingham village, on minor road off B6341 6m SW of Alnwick
Complex ruined castle, comprising a 13th-century hall-house, a defended courtyard of the 14th century and a large tower for domestic use added in the 15th century.
Open: Any reasonable time.
OS Map 81; ref NU 115092

Brinkburn Priory

Etal Castle

In Etal village, 8m SW of Berwick
Typical compact 14th-century Border castle, comprising 4-storey keep, gatehouse, parts of its curtain wall and corner tower.
Open: Any reasonable time.
Facilities: 🅿 Toilets (in village)
OS Map 75; ref NT 925394

Hadrian's Wall

See pages 52–56

● Lindisfarne Priory

On Holy Island, which can be reached at low tide across a causeway. Tide tables are posted at each end of the causeway
Ruins of 11th-century Benedictine priory on the presumed site of a religious house founded by St Aidan in 635, later the seat of the bishopric of the Northumbrian Kingdom until destroyed by the Danes in 875. Museum contains exciting exhibition and souvenir shop.
Open: All year (subject to tide times). £1.40/£1.05/70p.
Facilities: Souvenir shop, toilets 🅿
Tel: (028989) 200
OS Map 75; ref NU 126418

Lindisfarne Priory

● Norham Castle

Norham village, 6½m SW of Berwick-upon-Tweed on minor road off B6470 (from A698)
One of the strongest of the Border castles, built *c.*1160 and much altered thereafter, but still retaining the ruins of a fine Norman keep.
Open: All year. 85p/65p/40p.
Facilities: ♿ (excluding keep)
Tel: (028982) 329
OS Map 75; ref NT 907476

Norham Castle

● Prudhoe Castle

In Prudhoe, on minor road off A695
Extensive remains of 12th-century castle with gatehouse, curtain wall and keep enclosed within surrounding earthworks and walls. Part of the inner ward is occupied by an early 19th-century 'gothick' house containing an exhibition about Prudhoe Castle and a video on Northumberland castles.
Open: All year. £1.15/85p/60p.
Facilities: Education room, souvenir shop, toilets 🅿 🐾
Tel: (0661) 33459
OS Map 88; ref NZ 092634

◗ Warkworth Castle and Hermitage

7½m S of Alnwick on A1068

Magnificent 15th-century keep, restored by Anthony Salvin in 19th century, amidst ruins dating from the 12th century. 14th-century hermitage upstream with a tiny chapel cut into the cliff beside the River Coquet.

Open: Castle: All year. 85p/65p/40p. Hermitage: Summer season, weekends only (access by boat ½m upstream). 60p/45p/30p.

Facilities: Toilets 🅿 at castle, ☕ 🎧 ♿ (castle, excluding keep)

Tel: (0665) 711423

OS Map 81; Castle ref NU 247057, Hermitage ref NU 242060

Warkworth Castle

Prudhoe Castle

Belsay Garden Tours

S ix fascinating natural history tours will be held in summer 1990, on themes including bats, insects, fungi and the breeding behaviour of birds. As places are limited, early booking is recommended; further details are available from the Head Custodian. Belsay Hall will also host a concert, a plant sale, a vintage car rally and a Teddy Bears' picnic in 1990.

English ⌗ Heritage

DURHAM

Piercebridge Roman Bridge

Stanwick Iron Age
Fortifications

Whitby Abbey

Richmond
Richmond Castle

Easby Abbey

Mount Grace Priory

Wheeldale
Roman Road

Scarborough

Scarborough Castle

Middleham Castle

Rievaulx Abbey

Pickering Castle

Marmion Tower

Byland
Abbey

Helmsley Castle

Studley Royal Church

Ripon

Aldborough Roman Town

Kirkham Priory

Wharram Percy
Church and
Deserted Medieval Village

Harrogate
Spofforth Castle

York

Clifford's Tower

HUMBERSIDE

Steeton Hall
Gateway

● **Aldborough Roman Town**
*¾m SE of Boroughbridge, on minor
road off B6265*
Capital of the Brigantes, the largest
tribe in Roman Britain. Remains include
parts of the Roman town wall and two
mosaic pavements. Museum features
finds from the site.
Open: Summer season. 85p/65p/40p.
Oct–Mar grounds only, admission free.
Facilities: Toilets (summer only) ☛
Tel: (0423) 322768
OS Map 99; ref SE 405667

Aldborough Roman Town

Byland Abbey
2m S of A170 between Thirsk and Helmsley, near Coxwold village
Cistercian abbey of great interest and beauty. The glazed floor tiles in the church are particularly well preserved. Exhibition of carved stones and other finds from the site.
Open: All year. 85p/65p/40p.
Facilities: ▣ Toilets ♿ (including toilet) Refreshments in Abbey Inn Tues–Sat 10.30am–2.30pm, Sun 11.45am–2.30pm.
Tel: (03476) 614
OS Map 100; ref SE 549789

Byland Abbey

● Easby Abbey
1m SE of Richmond off B6271
12th-century abbey of the Premonstratensian Order, with substantial remains of the monastic buildings and gatehouse.
Open: All year. 85p/65p/40p.
Facilities: ▣
OS Map 92; ref NZ 185003

Easby Abbey

● Helmsley Castle
Near town centre
12th-century castle with later additions including a 16th-century building with remains of original interiors. Spectacular earthwork defences. Exhibition and tableau on the history of the castle.
Open: All year. £1.15/85p/60p.
Facilities: ▣ (large car park north of castle)
Tel: (0439) 70442
OS Map 100; ref SE 611836

Helmsley Castle

● Kirkham Priory
5m SW of Malton on minor road off A64
Augustinian priory founded *c.*1125. The gatehouse has a remarkable display of late 13th-century heraldry.
Open: All year. 85p/65p/40p.
Facilities: ▣ ♿
Tel: (065381) 768
OS Map 100; ref SE 735657

Kirkham Priory

Marmion Tower

N of Ripon on A6108 in West Tanfield
Medieval gatehouse with upper chambers
and a particularly fine oriel window.
Open: All year.
OS Map 99; ref SE 267787

● Middleham Castle

At Middleham, 2m S of Leyburn on A6108
Massive 12th-century keep standing
within later fortifications and domestic
buildings. Childhood home of King Richard
III. Replica of the famous Middleham Jewel
on display.
Open: All year. 85p/65p/40p.
Facilities: Shop
Tel: (0969) 23899
OS Map 99; ref SE 128875

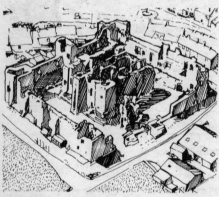

Middleham Castle

● Mount Grace Priory

7m NE of Northallerton on A19
near Ingleby Arncliffe
The finest example in Britain of a
monastery of the Carthusian Order,
founded in 1398. There are remains of
cloister, monastic church and outer court.
One monk's cell has been refurnished.
New exhibition in restored manor house.
Open: All year. £1.40/£1.05/70p.
Facilities: Education room, toilets 🅿 ⭘ ⊗ ♿
Tel: (0609) 83494
OS Map 99; ref SE 453982

● Pickering Castle

In Pickering, 15m SW of Scarborough
Fine motte-and-bailey castle with a
shell keep. Later curtain walls, towers,
domestic buildings and chapel. New
exhibition and souvenir shop opening 1991.
Open: All year. 85p/65p/40p.
Facilities: 🅿 ♿ (except motte)
Tel: (0751) 74989
OS Map 100; ref SE 800845

Pickering Castle

Piercebridge Roman Bridge

At Piercebridge, 4m W of
Darlington on B6275
Remains of southern abutment, washway
and portions of the piers carrying a
Roman timber bridge across the River
Tees in the 2nd century.
Open: Any reasonable time.
OS Map 93; ref NZ 214154

Mount Grace Priory

Richmond Castle
In Richmond
Splendid medieval fortress, with a
12th-century keep, one of the finest in the
country, and 11th-century remains of
curtain wall and domestic buildings. New
exhibition and souvenir shop opening
autumn 1990.
Open: All year. £1.15/85p/60p (prices
will increase when new visitor centre
opens).
Facilities: Toilets ⊕ ⊗ &
Tel: (0748) 2493
OS Map 92; ref NZ 174006

Richmond Castle

Rievaulx Abbey
*2¼m W of Helmsley on minor road
off B1257*
Cistercian abbey founded *c.*1132, in a
beautiful and secluded valley. The church
has the earliest large Cistercian nave in
Britain, while the choir is one of the finest
examples of 13th-century work, and there
are extensive remains of other monastic
buildings. Exhibition and souvenir shop.
Open: All year. £1.40/£1.05/70p.
Facilities: Education room, shop, toilets
⊕ P ♫ &
Tel: (04396) 228
OS Map 100; ref SE 577849

Rievaulx Abbey

Scarborough Castle
Castle Rd, E of town centre
12th-century castle with substantial
remains of a great rectangular keep
sited on a headland above the town and
commanding magnificent views. Remains
of 4th-century Roman signal station.
Open: All year. £1.15/85p/60p.
Facilities: Education room, toilets
⊕ ♫ & (except keep)
Tel: (0723) 372451
OS Map 101; ref TA 050893

Scarborough Castle

Spofforth Castle
*3½m SE of Harrogate, on minor
road off A661 at Spofforth*
Remains of the hall and solar wing of a
castle once in the possession of the
Percy family.
Open: All year.
OS Map 104; ref SE 360511

Stanwick Iron Age Fortifications
5m W of Darlington on B6275
Excavated section of the rampart and
rock-cut ditch of immense earthwork
enclosing an area of 850 acres.
Probably erected by the Brigantes as a
tribal rallying point at the time of
the Roman conquest.
Open: Any reasonable time.
OS Map 92; ref NZ 179112

Steeton Hall Gateway

4m NE of Castleford, on minor road
off A162 at South Milford
A small, well-preserved late
14th-century gatehouse.
Open: Any reasonable time. Key
available from Area Office.
Facilities: &
Tel: (0904) 658626
OS Map 105; ref SE 484314

Studley Royal: St Mary's Church

2½m W of Ripon off B6265, in grounds
of Studley Royal estate
Magnificent Victorian church designed by
William Burges in the 1870s. Original
decorations and fittings.
Open: Summer season, daily 1–5pm. The
Studley Royal estate, including Fountains
Abbey, is managed by the National Trust.
Estate tel. (076) 586 639.
Facilities: ◨ (National Trust) &
OS Map 99; ref SE 278703

Wharram Percy Church and Deserted Medieval Village

6m SE of Malton, on minor road from
B1248 ½m S of Wharram le Street
Ruined church and extensive earthworks
of deserted medieval village.
Open: Any reasonable time. Guided
tours of annual excavations in July.
Tel. Area Office for details (0904) 658626.
Facilities: ◨ at Bella Farm (¾m walk to
site)
OS Map 100; ref SE 859645

Wheeldale Roman Road

S of Goathland, W of A169, 7m S
of Whitby
Mile-long stretch of Roman road leading
north from the Roman camps at Cawthorn
and probably dating to the end of the
1st century AD.
Open: Any reasonable time.
OS Map 94; ref SE 805975

● Whitby Abbey

On cliff top E of Whitby town centre
The Benedictine church built in the
13th and 14th centuries dominates the
headland and stands on the site of the
monastery founded in 657, home of St Hilda
and Caedmon, the first English hymn
writer. Exhibition.
Open: All year. 85p/65p/40p.
Facilities: Toilets ◨ (both local council)
Tel: (0947) 603568
OS Map 94; ref NZ 904115

Whitby Abbey

● York: Clifford's Tower

In Castle St
13th-century tower on one of two mottes
thrown up by William the Conqueror in
1068–69 to hold York. Panoramic views of
city from top of the Tower. Some remains (not
in the care of English Heritage) of the
curtain wall and towers of the castle bailey
also survive behind Castle Museum.
Open: All year, plus Mondays in winter.
85p/65p/40p.
Facilities: ◨ (city council)
Tel: (0904) 646940
OS Map 105; ref SE 605515

Clifford's Tower

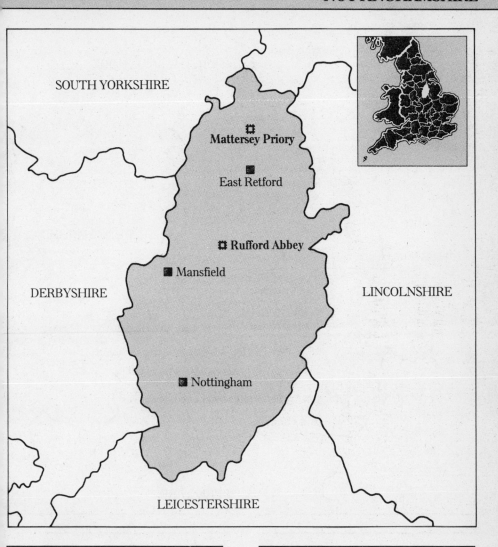

Mattersey Priory

1m E of Mattersey off B6045, 7m N of East Retford

Remains of small monastery of the Gilbertine Order founded in 1185.
Open: Any reasonable time.
OS Map 112; ref SK 704896

Rufford Abbey

2m S of Ollerton off A614

Remains of 12th-century Cistercian abbey and 17th-century country house. The abbey stands in Rufford Country Park, run by Nottinghamshire County Council.
Open: All year (closes 5pm in summer).
Facilities: Toilets 🅿 ✗ craft centre, shop ♿
Tel: (0623) 823148
OS Map 120; ref SK 645646

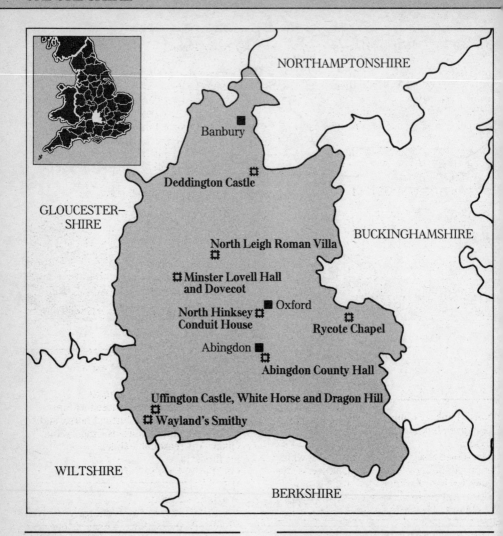

NORTHAMPTONSHIRE

Banbury

Deddington Castle

GLOUCESTER–
SHIRE

North Leigh Roman Villa

BUCKINGHAMSHIRE

Minster Lovell Hall
and Dovecot

North Hinksey
Conduit House

Oxford

Rycote Chapel

Abingdon

Abingdon County Hall

Uffington Castle, White Horse and Dragon Hill
Wayland's Smithy

WILTSHIRE

BERKSHIRE

Abingdon County Hall
*In Abingdon, 7m S of Oxford in Market
Place*
Fine 17th-century public building. It
was a Court for the Justices of Assize
and a Market Hall. Houses a museum with
displays on the geology, archaeology
and history of Abingdon.
Open: Museum open 1 Apr–31 Oct 1–5pm,
1 Nov–31 Mar 1–4pm. Closed Mon & Bank
Holidays.
OS Map 164; ref SU 497971

Deddington Castle
*S of B4031 on E side of Deddington,
17m N of Oxford on A423*
Extensive earthworks enclosing a large
outer and a small inner bailey.
Excavation has shown the latter to
contain remains of a 12th-century
curtain wall, hall and small rectangular
keep (these are not now visible).
Open: Any reasonable time.
OS Map 151; SP 471316

Minster Lovell Hall and Dovecot

*Adjacent to Minster Lovell church, 3m W
of Witney off A40*

Ruins of large 15th-century manor house
ranged round a quadrangle, including a
great hall with solar and kitchens. The
medieval dovecot survives with nesting
boxes complete.
Open: All year. 85p/65p/40p.
Facilities: 🅿
Tel: (0993) 75315
OS Map 164; ref SP 324114

Minster Lovell Hall

North Hinksey Conduit House

*In North Hinksey off A34, 2½m W of
Oxford*

The roofed reservoir for Oxford's first water
mains, built in the early 17th century. Water
collected here was piped to Carfax conduit.
Open: Any reasonable time (exterior only).
OS Map 164; ref SP 494054

North Leigh Roman Villa

*2m N of North Leigh, 9m W of Oxford off
A4095*

Remains of large villa on a site first
occupied in the 1st century. Its present
form was reached in the 4th century, and
remains include living quarters with mosaics
and baths, arranged round a courtyard.
Open: Summer season. 60p/45p/30p.
Pedestrian access only from main road
(600yds).
Tel: (0993) 881830
OS Map 164; ref SP 397154

● Rycote Chapel

3m SW of Thame off A329

Private chapel founded in 1449 which
retains its medieval font and pews as
well as two very fine 17th-century
roofed pews and other fittings.
Open: All year. 85p/65p/40p.
Facilities: 🅿 ⊗ ♿ (assistance required)
Tel: (08447) 346
OS Map 165; ref SP 667046

Rycote Chapel

Uffington Castle, White Horse and Dragon Hill

S of B4507, 7m W of Wantage

Large Iron Age camp enclosed within
ramparts and ditch; a turf-cut horse, and
a natural mound known as Dragon Hill.
Open: Any reasonable time.
Facilities: 🅿
OS Map 174; ref SU 301866

Wayland's Smithy

S of B4507, 8½m W of Wantage

Prehistoric burial place, a long earthen
mound covering a stone burial chamber.
Open: Any reasonable time.
OS Map 174; ref SU 281854

North Leigh Roman Villa

CHESHIRE

STAFFORDSHIRE

Old Oswestry
⬦ Hill Fort
■ Oswestry

Moreton Corbet Castle ⬦

Haughmond Abbey ⬦
Shrewsbury ■
Lilleshall Abbey ⬦

Wroxeter Roman City
⬦

Cantlop Bridge ⬦
Boscobel House ⬦
White Ladies Priory ⬦
Buildwas Abbey ⬦
Acton Burnell Castle ⬦
⬦ Iron Bridge
Langley Chapel ⬦
⬦
Mitchell's
Fold
Stone
Circle
⬦
Wenlock Priory

■ Bridgnorth

⬦ Stokesay Castle

■ Ludlow

HEREFORD AND WORCESTER

Acton Burnell Castle
In Acton Burnell, on unclassified
road 8m S of Shrewsbury
Fortified manor house, built by Robert
Burnell, Bishop of Bath and Wells,
towards the end of the 13th century.
Open: Any reasonable time.
Facilities: &
OS Map 126; ref SJ 534019

● **Boscobel House and the Royal Oak**
On unclassified road between A41 and
A5, 8m NW of Wolverhampton
Timber-framed hunting lodge (now fully
refurnished) built at the beginning of the
17th century, and attractively set among
later farm buildings. Best known for its
link with Charles II, who hid in the house
and a nearby oak tree after the Battle of
Worcester in 1651.
Open:All year(except Jan).£1.90/£1.50/95p.
Facilities: Exhibitions, education room,
souvenir shop, toilets ⓟ ✕ (weekends &
Bank Holidays only; other times by
arrangement)
& (gardens only)
Tel: (0902) 850244
OS Map 127; ref SJ 837083

Boscobel House

● **Buildwas Abbey**
On S bank of River Severn on B4378,
2m W of Iron Bridge
Cistercian abbey founded in 1135. The
extensive ruins date mostly from the
12th century, including the church which
is almost complete except for the roof.
Open: All year. 85p/65p/40p.
Facilities: &
Tel: (095245) 3274
OS Map 127; ref SJ 642044

Cantlop Bridge
¾m SW of Berrington on unclassified
road off A458
Single-span cast-iron road bridge over
the Cound Brook designed by Thomas
Telford.
Open: Any reasonable time.
OS Map 126; ref SJ 517062

● **Haughmond Abbey**
3m NE of Shrewsbury off B5062
Extensive remains of an abbey of
Augustinian canons, founded c.1135. The
church was demolished in 1539, but other
buildings survive including the chapter
house which retains its late medieval timber
ceiling. Fine medieval sculpture and
small exhibition.
Open: All year. 85p/65p/40p.
Facilities: ⓟ &
Tel: (074377) 661
OS Map 126; ref SJ 542152

Haughmond Abbey

Buildwas Abbey

Iron Bridge

In Iron Bridge, adjacent to A4169
The world's first iron bridge and
Britain's best-known industrial
monument, cast in Coalbrookdale by
local ironmaster Abraham Darby and
erected across the River Severn in
1779.
Open: Any reasonable time.
OS Map 127; ref SJ 672034

Langley Chapel

*1¹/₂m S of Acton Burnell, on
unclassified road off A49 9¹/₂m
S of Shrewsbury*
Medieval chapel restored in 1601.
The wooden fittings are a survival of a
17th-century Puritan church layout.
Open: All year.
Tel. Area Office: (0902) 765105
OS Map 126; ref SJ 538001

Lilleshall Abbey

*On unclassified road off A518, 4m N of
Oakengates*
Extensive and evocative ruins of an
abbey of Augustinian canons including
remains of the 12th- and 13th-century
church with an aisleless nave, and of
the cloister buildings.
Open: Any reasonable time.
OS Map 127; ref SJ 738142

Lilleshall Abbey

Mitchell's Fold Stone Circle

16m SW of Shrewsbury W of A488
Prehistoric stone circle 85ft in
diameter, consisting originally of some
30 stones of which 15 are now visible.
Open: Any reasonable time.
OS Map 137; ref SO 306984

Moreton Corbet Castle

*In Moreton Corbet off B5063,
7m NE of Shrewsbury*
Castle with a small 13th-century keep
and the ruins of a fine Elizabethan
house, captured in 1644 from Charles I's
supporters by Parliamentary forces.
Open: Any reasonable time.
Facilities: 🅿 ♿
OS Map 126; ref SJ 562232

Old Oswestry Hill Fort

*1m N of Oswestry, accessible from
unclassified road off A483*
Impressive Iron Age fort of 68 acres
defended by a series of five ramparts
with an elaborate western entrance and
unusual earthwork cisterns.
Open: Any reasonable time.
OS Map 126; ref SJ 295310

● Stokesay Castle

1m S of Craven Arms off A49
Superb example of a large and little
altered fortified manor house built in the
late 13th century, with early 17th-century
gatehouse. Well-preserved great hall and
fine timber fire surround in solar.
Open: 7 Mar–31 Oct, daily except
Tues 10am–6pm (5pm in Mar & Oct);
1–30 Nov open 10am–4pm weekends only,
and parties during the week by arrangement.
£1.50/75p (no reduction for OAPs,
students or unemployed)
Facilities: Toilets 🅿 🍽
♿ (gardens & great hall only)
Tel: (0588) 672544
OS Map 137; ref SO 436817

Wenlock Priory
In Much Wenlock
Ruins of large Cluniac priory in a
garden setting. Substantial remains of
early 13th-century church and Norman
chapter house.
Open: All year. 85p/65p/40p.
Facilities: 🅿 🎧
Tel: (0952) 727466
OS Map 127; ref SJ 625001

Wenlock Priory

White Ladies Priory
*1m SW of Boscobel House off unclassified
road between A41 and A5, 8m NW of
Wolverhampton*
Ruins of late 12th-century church of a
small priory of Augustinian canonesses,
converted to a house after the Dissolution.
Charles II hid here and in nearby woods
in 1651 before moving to Boscobel.
Open: Any reasonable time.
OS Map 127; ref SJ 826076

● Wroxeter Roman City
*At Wroxeter, 5m E of Shrewsbury
1m S of A5*
Civic centre of the Roman town of
Viroconium. Excavated remains of the 2nd-
century municipal baths are displayed.
Site museum has finds from the town and
earlier legionary fortress.
Open: All year. 85p/65p/40p.
Facilities: Education room, shop 🅿 ♿
Tel: (074375) 330
OS Map 126; ref SJ 568088

Wroxeter Roman City

Stokesay Castle

For full details of
opening times see page 4

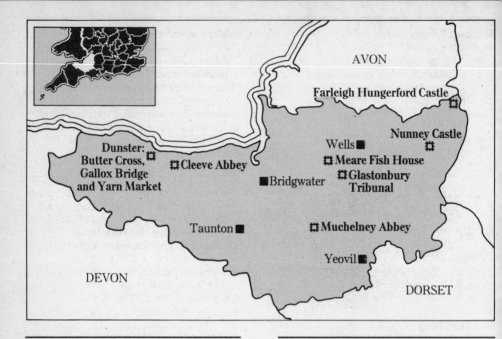

Cleeve Abbey
In Washford, ¼m S of A39
Ruins of a Cistercian abbey founded in
the very late 12th century. Little remains of
the church but many of the claustral
buildings survive including the frater
with its fine timber roof. Exhibition.
Open: All year. £1.15/85p/60p.
Facilities: Toilets 🅿 🚌 🚫
& (grounds & ground floor only)
Tel: (0984) 40377
OS Map 181; ref ST 047407

Cleeve Abbey

Dunster: Butter Cross
*Beside the minor road to Alcombe,
400yd NW of Dunster Parish church*
Medieval stone cross, also known as
Rockhead Cross, said to have been sited
originally in the High Street.
Open: Any reasonable time.
OS Map 181; ref SS 988439

Dunster: Gallox Bridge
Off A396 at S end of Dunster
Medieval stone packhorse bridge with
two ribbed arches.
Open: Any reasonable time.
Facilities: &
OS Map 181; ref SS 990432

Dunster: Yarn Market
In Dunster High St
Octagonal market hall built in 1609 and
repaired in 1647, used for the sale of
locally woven cloth.
Open: Any reasonable time.
Facilities: &
OS Map 181; ref SS 992437

● **Farleigh Hungerford Castle**
In Farleigh Hungerford 3¹/2m W of
Trowbridge on A366
Late 14th-century castle with large
15th-century outer court. The chapel
contains the fine tomb of Sir Thomas
Hungerford, builder of the castle.
Open: All year. 85p/65p/40p.
Facilities: Toilets 🅿️ ⊗ ♿ (exterior only)
Tel: (0272) 734472
OS Map 173; ref ST 801577

Farleigh Hungerford Castle

● **Glastonbury Tribunal**
In Glastonbury High St
The 15th-century abbey courthouse,
refaced 1493–1524 and later converted
into a private dwelling house. Site museum.
Open: All year. 85p/65p/40p.
Facilities: ⊗ ♿ (ground floor only – 2 steps)
Tel: (0458) 32949
OS Map 182; ref ST 499390

Glastonbury Tribunal

Meare Fish House
In Meare village on B3151
A small stone first floor hill house,
probably erected in the 14th century for the
abbey official in charge of the fisheries.
Open: Any reasonable time. Key from
Manor House farm.
OS Map 182; ref ST 458418

● **Muchelney Abbey**
In Muchelney 2m S of Langport
Benedictine abbey founded about AD950.
Excavated ground plan of the later abbey
church and well-preserved remains of
the 15th-century south cloister range and
abbot's lodging, later used as a farmhouse.
Open: Summer season. 85p/65p/40p.
Facilities: Toilets 🅿️ ⊗
♿ (part of ground floor only)
Tel: (0458) 250664
OS Map 193; ref ST 428248

Muchelney Abbey

Nunney Castle
In Nunney 3¹/2m SW of Frome, off A361
Small 14th-century castle in the French
style, consisting of a central block with
large round towers at the angles, closely
confined within a moat.
Open: Any reasonable time.
Facilities: ♿ (exterior only)
OS Map 183; ref ST 737457

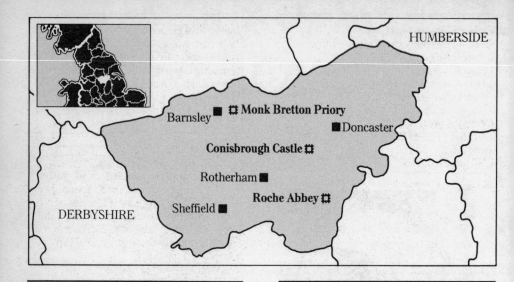

Barnsley ■ ⚏ **Monk Bretton Priory**

■**Doncaster**

Conisbrough Castle ⚏

Rotherham ■

Roche Abbey ⚏

Sheffield ■

HUMBERSIDE

DERBYSHIRE

● **Conisbrough Castle**
NE of Conisbrough town centre
off A630, 4½m SW of Doncaster
One of the finest 12th-century keeps in
England, featured in Sir Walter Scott's
novel *Ivanhoe*. Later curtain wall with
solid round towers. New visitor centre
and exhibition.
Open: All year. £1.15/85p/60p. (The castle
is in the care of English Heritage and
administered by the Ivanhoe Trust.)
Facilities: 🅿 ♿ (limited access)
Tel: (0709) 863329
OS Map 111; ref SK 515989

Conisbrough Castle

● Monk Bretton Priory

1m E of Barnsley town centre off A633
A Cluniac priory founded in 1153.
Extensive remains of the gatehouse,
west range and other buildings.
Open: All year. 60p/45p/30p.
Facilities: Toilets (summer season) 🅿 &
Tel: (0226) 204089
OS Map 111; ref SE 373065

Monk Bretton Priory

● Roche Abbey

1½m S of Maltby off A634
Cistercian abbey founded in 1147. The
walls of the church transepts still
stand to their full height, and
excavation has revealed the complete
layout of the monastic buildings. Small
exhibition traces the history of the Abbey.
Open: Summer season, daily; Winter,
weekends only, 10am–4pm. £1.15/85p/60p
(includes free audio tour).
Facilities: Toilets 🅿 ⬗ ⌒ &
Tel: (0709) 812739
OS Map 111; ref SK 544898

Roche Abbey

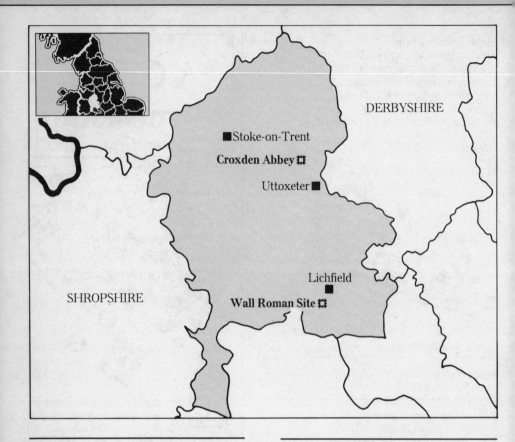

DERBYSHIRE

■Stoke-on-Trent
Croxden Abbey ✜

Uttoxeter ■

SHROPSHIRE

Lichfield ■
Wall Roman Site ✜

Croxden Abbey
3m NW of Uttoxeter off A50
Cistercian abbey founded in 1176. The
east range of the cloisters survives as do the
west front and south transept of the church.
Open: Any reasonable time.
OS Map 128; ref SK 065397

● **Wall Roman Site (Letocetum)**
Off A5 at Wall near Lichfield
Remains of public baths and lodging house
of a small settlement on Watling Street,
the best-preserved remains of any small
Roman roadside settlement. Small site
museum.
Open: All year. 85p/65p/40p. (NT)
Facilities: ⌒
Tel:(0543) 480768
OS Map 139; ref SK 099067

Wall Roman Site

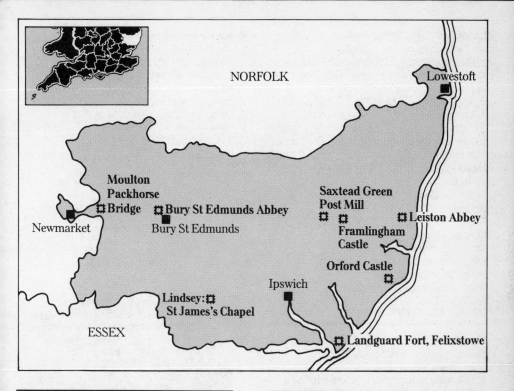

NORFOLK

Lowestoft

Moulton
Packhorse
Bridge   Bury St Edmunds Abbey

Saxtead Green
Post Mill

Leiston Abbey

Newmarket

Bury St Edmunds

Framlingham
Castle

Orford Castle

Ipswich

Lindsey:
St James's Chapel

ESSEX

Landguard Fort, Felixstowe

Bury St Edmunds Abbey
E end of town centre
Remains of the Benedictine abbey
including the Romanesque and 14th-century
gatehouses (exteriors only), and substantial
parts of the church, including the
crossing, transepts and crypt.
Open: Park opening hours (borough
council).
OS Map 155; ref TL 858642

● Framlingham Castle
In Framlingham on B1116
Massive walls and towers of a castle of
*c.*1200. The 18th-century Poor House
occupies the site of the Great Hall of the
castle. Local museum (extra charge).
Open: All year. £1.15/85p/60p.
Facilities: Education room, shop 🅿 🍴
♿ (grounds & ground floor only)
Tel: (0728) 723330/724189
OS Map 156; ref TM 287637

Framlingham Castle

Landguard Fort, Felixstowe
1m S of Felixstowe near docks
18th-century fort, with impressive 19th-
and 20th-century additions, built on the
site of earlier forts. Site museum.
Open: 27 May–30 Sept Wed, Thur & Sun
2.30–5pm. Guided tours Wed & Sun
2.45pm & 4pm. 80p/50p (no unaccompanied
children or concessionary rates). For further
information tel. Mrs D Rayner (Felixstowe
Historical Society): (0394) 286403
(evenings).
Facilities: 🅿 🍽
OS Map 169; ref TM 284318

Leiston Abbey
1m N of Leiston off B1069
Extensive remains of an abbey for
Premonstratensian canons.
Open: Any reasonable time.
Facilities: 🅿 &
OS Map 156; ref TM 445642

Lindsey: St James's Chapel
On unclassified road 1/2m E of
Rose Green, 8m E of Sudbury
13th-century chapel with lancet windows
and piscina but incorporating earlier work.
Open: All year.
Facilities: & (single step)
OS Map 155; ref TL 978443

Moulton Packhorse Bridge
In Moulton off B1085, 4m E of Newmarket
Medieval bridge on ancient route from
Bury St Edmunds to Cambridge.
Open: Any reasonable time.
Facilities: 🅿 &
OS Map 154; ref TL 698645

⬤ Orford Castle
In Orford on B1084 20m NE of Ipswich
A royal castle built for coastal defence
1165–72. A magnificent keep survives,
standing almost intact to a height of 90ft.
Local topographical display in keep.
Open: All year. £1.15/85p/60p.
Facilities: 🅿
Tel: (03944) 50472
OS Map 169; ref TM 419499

⬤ Saxtead Green Post Mill
2 1/2m NW of Framlingham on A1120
Four-sailed corn mill, with a
19th-century wooden superstructure
mounted on a brick round-house.
In working order.
Open: Summer season, Mon–Sat
10am–6pm. 85p/65p/40p.
Tel: (0728) 82789
OS Map 156; ref TM 253645

Saxtead Green Post Mill

Orford Castle

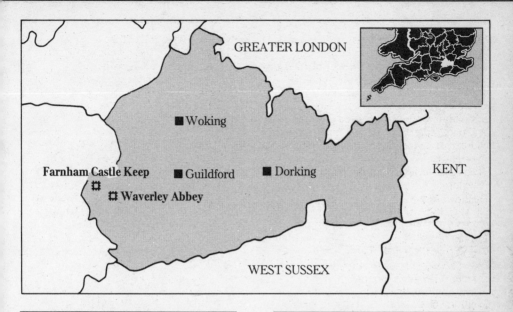

GREATER LONDON

■ Woking

Farnham Castle Keep

■ Guildford ■ Dorking

KENT

✜ **Waverley Abbey**

WEST SUSSEX

● **Farnham Castle Keep**
½m N of Farnham town centre on A287
Motte-and-bailey castle, former residence
of the Bishops of Winchester, with a large
shell-keep enclosing a mound in which are
massive foundations of a Norman tower.
Open: Summer season. £1.15/85p/60p
(includes free audio tour).
Facilities: 🅿 👂
Tel: (0252) 713393
OS Map 186; ref SU 839474

Waverley Abbey
2m SE of Farnham off B3001
The earliest Cistercian house in
England, founded in 1128 by Bishop
Gifford. The upstanding remains mostly
date from the 13th century.
Open: Any reasonable time.
Facilities: 🅿 (limited)
OS Map 186; ref SU 868453

Farnham Castle Keep

SURREY　　　　**KENT**

■ Horsham　　**Bayham Abbey** ✚

WEST SUSSEX　　## EAST SUSSEX

✚ **Battle Abbey**

Bramber Castle ✚

■ Chichester　　**Pevensey Castle** ✚　■ Hastings

Brighton　　■ Eastbourne

● Battle Abbey and Site of the Battle of Hastings

At S end of Battle High St

Remains of the abbey founded by William the Conqueror on the site of the Battle of Hastings, including a splendid gatehouse and claustral buildings including the fine east range. The impressive battlefield can also be visited.

Open: All year, plus Mondays in winter.

£1.70/£1.30/85p.

Facilities: Visitor centre, including audiovisual – '1066, The Battle of Hastings' and shop; Abbot's Hall open to public school summer holidays only; toilets.

🅿 🍴 🎧 ♿ (some steps)

Tel: (04246) 3792

OS Map 199; ref TQ 749157

Battle Abbey

Bayham Abbey

1¾m W of Lamberhurst off B2169
Impressive riverside ruins of a house
of Premonstratensian canons, founded
*c.*1208 and preserved in the
18th century to provide a romantic
vista for the nearby 'gothick' house.
Open: Summer season.
85p/65p/40p.
Facilities: Toilets ℗ ఉ
Tel: (0892) 890381
OS Map 188; ref TQ 651366

Bayham Abbey

Bramber Castle

*On W side of Bramber village off
A283*
Remains of Norman motte-and-bailey
castle with later additions, dramatically
sited to guard the Adur valley.
Open: Any reasonable time. (NT)
Facilities: ℗ (limited)
OS Map 198; ref TQ 187107

Pevensey Castle

In Pevensey
Medieval castle, including the remains of an
unusual keep, enclosed within the walls
of the 4th-century Roman fort Anderida.
Open: All year. £1.15/85p/60p.
Facilities: ℗ ఉ (Toilets nearby)
Tel: (0323) 762604
OS Map 199; ref TQ 645048

Pevensey Castle

**For full details of
opening times see page 4**

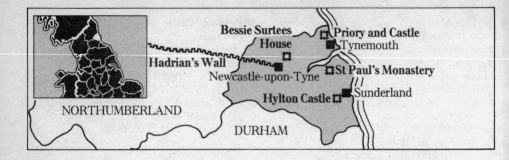

Hadrian's Wall *See pages 52–56*

Bessie Surtees House
41–44 Sandhill, Newcastle
English Heritage, Properties in Care,
North Region Headquarters
Two 16th and 17th century merchants'
houses on the quayside near the Tyne
Bridge. One half-timbered, one re-fronted in
brick *c.*1721. Principal rooms on view.
Exhibitions about the property and the work
of English Heritage.
Open: All year, plus Mondays in winter.
Facilities: Souvenir shop, toilets
Tel: (091) 261 1585
OS Map 88; ref NZ 252639

● Hylton Castle
3³/₄m W of Sunderland
Much-altered keep-gatehouse built in the
early 15th century, retaining a fine display
of medieval heraldry. The 15th–16th-
century St Catherine's Chapel with
half-octagonal transepts stands nearby.
Open: All year. 60p/45p/30p.
Facilities: ▣ ⅙ (grounds only)
OS Map 88; ref NZ 358588

St Paul's Monastery, Jarrow
In Jarrow, on minor road N of A185
Founded 682, home of the Venerable
Bede, re-founded in 1075; parts of Bede's
church survive as the chancel of the parish
church. Exhibition in Jarrow Hall open free
to EH members.
Open: Any reasonable time.
Facilities: ⅙
OS Map 88; ref NZ 339652

● Tynemouth Castle and Priory
In Tynemouth, near North Pier
Castle walls and gatehouse enclose the
substantial remains of a Benedictine priory
founded 1090 on a Saxon monastic site.
Latterly coastal batteries, now containing
reconstructed World War I magazine, were
mounted here to defend the entrance to
the Tyne.
Open: All year; Gun battery exhibition
open pm Fri–Mon. 85p/65p/40p.
Facilities: Souvenir shop, toilets (local
council) ⅙ (castle)
Tel: (091) 257 1090
OS Map 88; ref NZ 374695

Tynemouth Priory

STAFFORDSHIRE

WEST MIDLANDS

Rugby

⊞ Kenilworth Castle

◼ Warwick

◼ Stratford-upon-Avon

NORTHAMPTONSHIRE

HEREFORD
AND WORCESTER

● **Kenilworth Castle**
In Kenilworth
One of the finest and most extensive
castles in Britain. Remains date from the
12th to the 17th centuries, including a keep
and great hall behind gatehouse, curtain
walls, outworks and water defences.
Site exhibition.
Open: All year. £1.15/85p/60p.
Facilities: Education room, toilets 🅿 ♿ 🎧
Tel: (0926) 52078
OS Map 140; ref SP 278723

Kenilworth Castle

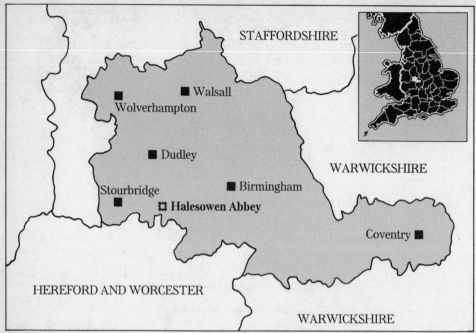

STAFFORDSHIRE

■ Walsall

Wolverhampton ■

■ Dudley

Stourbridge ■

■ Birmingham

⬚ **Halesowen Abbey**

WARWICKSHIRE

Coventry ■

HEREFORD AND WORCESTER

WARWICKSHIRE

● **Halesowen Abbey**
Off A456 Kidderminster road, 6m W of Birmingham city centre
Remains of abbey founded in 1215 by King John. Parts of the church can be seen together with what was probably the monks' infirmary.
Open: 2 June–1 Sept, weekends & Bank Holidays only 10am–6pm. 50p/35p/25p.
Facilities: ▣ ♿(rough grass between church and infirmary)
OS Map 139; ref SO 975828

Halesowen Abbey

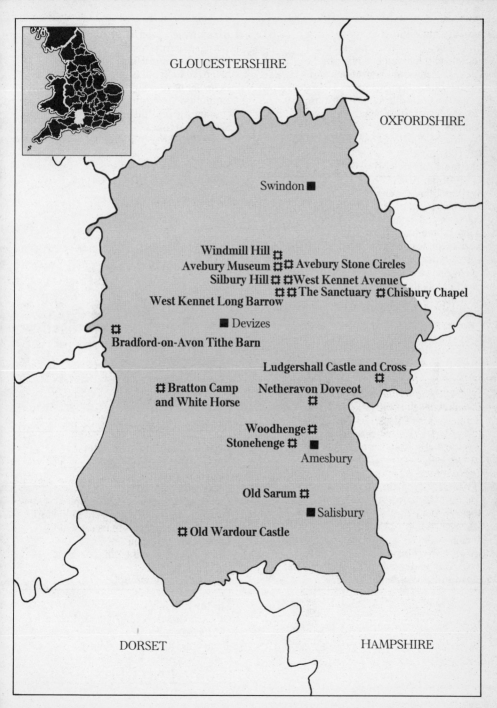

GLOUCESTERSHIRE

OXFORDSHIRE

Swindon ■

Windmill Hill ✜
Avebury Museum ✜ ✜ Avebury Stone Circles
Silbury Hill ✜ ✜ West Kennet Avenue
✜ ✜ The Sanctuary ✜ Chisbury Chapel
West Kennet Long Barrow

■ Devizes

✜
Bradford-on-Avon Tithe Barn

Ludgershall Castle and Cross
✜

✜ Bratton Camp   Netheravon Dovecot
and White Horse   ✜

Woodhenge ✜
Stonehenge ✜   ■
Amesbury

Old Sarum ✜
■ Salisbury

✜ Old Wardour Castle

DORSET   HAMPSHIRE

● Avebury Museum
In Avebury 7m W of Marlborough
Founded by Alexander Keiller in the
1930s, the museum houses one of the
most important prehistoric
archaeological collections in Britain.
Open: All year, plus Mondays in winter.
85p/65p/40p.
Facilities: Education room, toilets 🅿 ⊗ ♿
Tel: (06723) 250
OS Map 173; ref SU 100700

Avebury Stone Circles
In Avebury 7m W of Marlborough
Complex and gigantic late Neolithic
henge monument with remains of the
original stone circles enclosed within
a great outer ditch and circle.
Open: Any reasonable time. (NT)
Facilities: Toilets 🅿 ♿
OS Map 173; ref SU 103700

Avebury Stone Circles

Avebury
See also The Sanctuary, Silbury Hill,
West Kennet Avenue (NT), West Kennet Long
Barrow and Windmill Hill (NT)

● Bradford-on-Avon Tithe Barn
¼m S of town centre, off B3109
Fine 14th-century barn which formerly
belonged to Shaftesbury Abbey, a
Benedictine nunnery. Now houses an
exhibition illustrating farming and
country life in Wiltshire in Victorian and
Edwardian times.
Open: Tel. Area Office for details:
(0272) 734472.
Facilities: 🅿 ♿
OS Map 173; ref ST 824604

Bradford-on-Avon Tithe Barn

Bratton Camp and White Horse
2m E of Westbury off B3098,
1m SW of Bratton
Large Iron Age hill fort (*c.*300BC–
AD43), enclosing a Neolithic long
barrow. The White Horse cut in the turf
below the camp dates in its present
form to the 18th century.
Open: Any reasonable time.
Facilities: 🅿
OS Map 184; ref ST 900516

Chisbury Chapel
On unclassified road off A4 6m E
of Marlborough
Thatched 13th-century chapel.
Open: Any reasonable time.
OS Map 174; ref SU 280658

Ludgershall Castle and Cross
On N side of Ludgershall off A342
Royal castle dating from the early
12th century, which had become a royal
hunting palace by the 13th century but
was a ruin by the 15th and 16th
centuries. The late medieval cross
stands in the main street of the village.
Open: Any reasonable time.
Facilities: **P** (limited) & (part of site only
& Village Cross)
OS Map 184; ref SU 264513

Netheravon Dovecot
In Netheravon, 4½m N of Amesbury on A345
Early 18th-century brick dovecot
retaining most of its more than 700
stone-built chalk nesting boxes.
Open: Exterior viewing only, by written
application to PIC (SW), Keysign House,
429 Oxford Street, London W1R 2HD.
OS Map 184; ref SU 146485

● Old Sarum
2m N of Salisbury off A345
An Iron Age hill fort in origin and
thereafter a Roman settlement, a Saxon
burh, a Norman motte, castle and town,
and the site of the first Salisbury
Cathedral and palace of the bishop,
begun in 1078 and abandoned in 1226.
Open: All year. 85p/65p/40p.
Facilities: Toilets **P**
& (inner bailey & grounds only)
Tel: (0722) 335398
OS Map 184; ref SU 138327

Old Sarum

● Old Wardour Castle
Off A30 2m SW of Tisbury
Hexagonal castle built *c.*1393 round a
central courtyard, with 16th-century
alterations in Renaissance style. Badly
damaged during the Civil War, but
preserved in the 18th century as a
landscape feature. Site exhibitions.
Open: Summer season, daily;
winter, weekends only, 10am–4pm.
85p/65p/40p.
Facilities: Toilets **P** & (grounds only)
Tel: (0747) 870487
OS Map 184; ref ST 939263

Old Wardour Castle

The Sanctuary, Overton Hill, Avebury
Beside A4, ½m E of West Kennet
Prehistoric monument, probably late
Neolithic, consisting of two concentric
circles of stones and six of timber
uprights indicated by concrete stumps,
connected to Avebury by the West Kennet
Avenue of standing stones.
Open: Any reasonable time.
OS Map 173; ref SU 118679

Silbury Hill
1m W of West Kennet on A4
Artificial prehistoric mound, the largest
existing example of this type in Europe and
probably dating from the late Neolithic Age.
Open: Any reasonable time (no access
to the Hill itself).
Facilities: **P** & (viewing area)
OS Map 173; ref SU 100685

Stonehenge

● Stonehenge
*2m W of Amesbury on junction of A303
and A344/A360*
Britain's most famous prehistoric
monument, dating from between 3100 and
1100 BC, and consisting of a series of
concentric stone circles, surrounded by
a ditch and bank, and approached by an
'avenue'.
Open: All year, plus Mondays in
winter. £1.70/£1.30/85p. (NT)
Facilities: Souvenir shop, toilets 🅿 ✕ ⊗ ♿
Tel: (0980) 623108
OS Map 184; ref SU 123422

West Kennet Avenue, Avebury
Leading alongside B4003
Avenue of standing stones, some re-erected,
probably dating from the late Neolithic Age.
Open: Any reasonable time. (NT)
Facilities: ♿ (on roadway)
OS Map 173; ref SU 105695

West Kennet Long Barrow
¾m SW of West Kennet along footpath off A4
Neolithic long barrow, a burial place
consisting of a long earthen mound
containing a passage with side chambers
for human remains, and with the
entrance blocked by a large stone.
Open: Any reasonable time.
Facilities: 🅿 (in layby)
OS Map 173; ref SU 104677

Windmill Hill
1½m NW of Avebury
Neolithic 'causewayed camp' of
uncertain purpose, possibly a market or
tribal centre. Excavated in the 1920s
when the finds were placed in the
Avebury Museum.
Open: Any reasonable time. (NT)
OS Map 173; ref SU 086714

Woodhenge
*1½m N of Amesbury, off A345 just S of
Durrington*
Neolithic henge monument of *c.*2300BC,
consisting of six rings of timber
posts, now marked by concrete stumps,
surrounded by a ditch and entered by a
causeway. The long axis of the rings,
which are oval, points to the rising
sun on Midsummer Day.
Open: Any reasonable time.
Facilities: 🅿 ♿
OS Map 184; ref SU 151434

Abbotsbury Abbey Remains 37
Abbotsbury: St Catherine's Chapel 38
Abingdon County Hall 98
Acton Burnell Castle 101
Agricola Tower and Castle Walls, Chester 22
Aldborough Roman Town 92
Ambleside Roman Fort 27
Appuldurcombe House 66
Arbor Low Stone Circle & Gib Hill Barrow 31
Arthur's Round Table 27
Arthur's Stone, Dorstone 61
Ashby de la Zouch Castle 77
Auckland Castle Deer House, Bishop Auckland 39
Audley End House and Park 41
Avebury Museum 118
Avebury Stone Circles 118
Avebury: The Sanctuary 120
Aydon Castle 88

Baconsthorpe Castle 81
Ballowall Barrow, St Just 24
Banks East Turret 53
Banqueting House 46
Bant's Carn Burial Chamber and Halangy Down Ancient Village 68
Barnard Castle 39
Barrow-in-Furness: Bow Bridge 28
Barton-upon-Humber: St Peter's Church 64
Battle Abbey and site of the Battle of Hastings 112
Bayard's Cove Fort 33
Bayham Abbey 113
Beeston Castle 22
Belas Knap Long Barrow 43
Belsay Hall, Castle and Gardens 88
Benwell Roman Temple 53
Benwell Vallum Crossing 53
Berkhamsted Castle 63
Berney Arms Windmill 81
Berry Pomeroy Castle 34
Berwick-upon-Tweed: Berwick Barracks 88
Berwick-upon-Tweed Castle 89
Berwick-upon-Tweed Ramparts 89
Bessie Surtees House 114
Binham Priory 82
Binham Wayside Cross 82

Birdoswald Fort, Wall and Turret 53
Bishop Auckland: Auckland Castle Deer House 39
Bishop's Palace, Lincoln 80
Bishop's Waltham Palace 57
Blackbury Camp 33
Black Carts Turret 33
Blackfriars, Gloucester 43
Black Middens Bastle House 89
Blakeney Guildhall 82
Bolingbroke Castle 79
Bolsover Castle 32
Boscobel House and the Royal Oak 101
Bow Bridge, Barrow-in-Furness 28
Bowes Castle 40
Bradford-on-Avon Tithe Barn 118
Bramber Castle 113
Bratton Camp and White Horse 118
Brinkburn Priory 89
Bristol: Temple Church 16
Brougham Castle 28
Brougham: Countess Pillar 28
Brough Castle 38
Brunton Turret 53
Buildwas Abbey 101
Burgh Castle 82
Burton Agnes Manor House 64
Bury St Edmunds Abbey 109
Bushmead Priory 17
Butter Cross, Dunster 104
Byland Abbey 93

Caister Roman Site 82
Callington: Dupath Well 24
Calshot Castle 58
Canterbury: St Augustine's Abbey 74
Cantlop Bridge 101
Carisbrooke Castle 66
Carlisle Castle 28
Carn Euny Ancient Village 24
Carrawburgh: Temple of Mithras 54
Castle Acre Bailey Gate 82
Castle Acre Castle 82
Castle Acre Priory 82
Castlerigg Stone Circle 29
Castle Rising Castle 83
Cawfields Roman Wall and Milecastle 54
Chester Castle: Agricola Tower and Castle Walls 22
Chester Roman Amphitheatre 22
Chesters Bridge Abutment 54

Chesters Fort and Museum   54
Chichele College   85
Chisbury Chapel   118
Chiswick House   47
Christchurch Castle and Norman
   House   37
Church of the Holy Sepulchre,
   Thetford   84
Chysauster Ancient Village   24
Cirencester Amphitheatre   43
Cleeve Abbey   104
Clifford's Tower, York   96
Clifton Hall   29
Colchester: Lexden Straight Road and
   Bluebottle Grove Earthworks   41
Colchester: St Botolph's Priory   42
Colchester: St John's Abbey Gate   42
Conisbrough Castle   106
Coombe Conduit   47
Corbridge Roman Site   54
Countess Pillar, Brougham   28
Cow Tower, Norwich   84
Creake Abbey   83
Cromwell's Castle   69
Croxden Abbey   108

Dartmouth: Bayard's Cove Fort   33
Dartmouth Castle   34
Deal Castle   70
Deddington Castle   98
Deerhurst: Odda's Chapel   44
De Grey Mausoleum   18
Denny Abbey   20
Denton Hall Turret and West Denton   55
Donnington Castle   19
Dorstone: Arthur's Stone   61
Dover Castle   71
Dover: Knights Templar Church   71
Dragon Hill   99
Dunstanburgh Castle   89
Dunster: Butter Cross   104
Dunster: Gallox Bridge   104
Dunster: Yarn Market   104
Dupath Well, Callington   24
Duxford Chapel   21
Dymchurch Martello Tower no 24   72

Easby Abbey   93
Ebbsfleet: St Augustine's Cross   74
Edlingham Castle   89
Edvin Loach Old Church   61

Egglestone Abbey   40
Eleanor Cross, Geddington   85
Eltham Palace   47
Etal Castle   90
Eyam Moor Tumulus and Stone Circle   32
Eynsford Castle   72

Farleigh Hungerford Castle   105
Farnham Castle Keep   112
Faversham Stone Chapel   72
Felixstowe: Landguard Fort   110
Fiddleford Manor   37
Finchale Priory   40
Flowerdown Barrows   58
Fort Brockhurst   58
Fowey: St Catherine's Castle   26
Framlingham Castle   109
Furness Abbey   29

Gainsborough Old Hall   79
Gainsthorpe Deserted Medieval
   Village   64
Gallox Bridge, Dunster   104
Garrison Church, Portsmouth   59
Garrison Walls   68
Geddington: Eleanor Cross   85
Gilsland Vicarage Roman Wall   55
Gisborough Priory   23
Glastonbury Tribunal   105
Gloucester, Blackfriars   43
Gloucester, Greyfriars   44
Goodrich Castle   61
Goodshaw Chapel   76
Grange, The, Northington   58
Gravesend: Milton Chantry   72
Great Witcombe Roman Villa   44
Great Yarmouth: Greyfriars' Cloister   83
Great Yarmouth: Old Merchant's House
   and Row 111 Houses   83
Greyfriars' Cloister, Great Yarmouth   83
Greyfriars, Gloucester   44
Grime's Graves   83
Grimspound   34

Hadleigh Castle   42
Hailes Abbey   44
Halesowen Abbey   116
Halliggye Fogou   25
Hampton Court Palace   47
Hardknott Roman Fort   29
Hardwick Old Hall   32

Hare Hill   55
Harrow's Scar Milecastle   55
Harry's Walls   68
Hastings, site of Battle of   112
Haughmond Abbey   101
Heddon-on-the-Wall   55
Helmsley Castle   93
Hetty Pegler's Tump (Uley Long
   Barrow)   45
Hob Hurst's House   32
Horne's Place Chapel, Appledore   72
Houghton House   18
Hound Tor Deserted Medieval
   Village   34
Housesteads Roman Fort   55
Hurlers Stone Circle   25
Hurst Castle   58
Hylton Castle   114

Innisidgen Lower and Upper Burial
   Chambers   68
Iron Bridge   102
Isleham Priory Church   21

Jarrow: St Paul's Monastery   114
Jewel Tower, Westminster   48
Jewry Wall, Leicester   78
Jordan Hill Roman Temple,
   Weymouth   37

Kempley: St Mary's Church   44
Kenilworth Castle   115
Kensington Palace   48
Kenwood   48
Kew Palace   49
King Charles's Castle   69
King Doniert's Stone, St Cleer   25
King James's and Landport Gates,
   Portsmouth   59
Kingston Russell Stone Circle   37
Kingswood Abbey Gatehouse   44
Kirby Hall   86
Kirby Muxloe Castle   77
Kirkham House, Paignton   35
Kirkham Priory   93
Kit's Coty House and Little Kit's Coty
   House   72
Knights Templar Church, Dover   71
Knowlton Church and Earthworks   38

Landguard Fort, Felixstowe   110

Lanercost Priory   29
Langley Chapel   102
Launceston Castle   25
Leahill Turret   55
Leicester: Jewry Wall   78
Leigh Court Barn   62
Leiston Abbey   110
Letocetum (Wall Roman Site)   108
Lexden Straight Road and Bluebottle
   Grove Earthworks, Colchester   41
Lilleshall Abbey   102
Lincoln: Bishop's Palace   80
Lindisfarne Priory   90
Lindsey: St James's Chapel   110
Little Kit's Coty House   72
London Wall, Tower Hill   49
Longthorpe Tower   21
Longtown Castle   62
Ludgershall Castle and Cross   119
Lullingstone Roman Villa   72
Lyddington Bede House   78
Lydford Castles and Saxon Town   35

Maiden Castle   38
Maison Dieu, Ospringe   73
Manaton: Hound Tor Deserted
   Medieval Village   34
Marble Hill House   49
Marmion Tower   94
Mattersey Priory   97
Mayburgh Earthwork   30
Meare Fish House   105
Medieval Merchant's House,
   Southampton   60
Merrivale Prehistoric Settlement   35
Middleham Castle   94
Milton Chantry, Gravesend   72
Minster Lovell Hall and Dovecot   99
Mistley Towers   42
Mitchell's Fold Stone Circle   102
Monk Bretton Priory   107
Moreton Corbet Castle   102
Mortimer's Cross Water Mill   62
Moulton Packhorse Bridge   110
Mount Batten Tower   35
Mount Grace Priory   94
Muchelney Abbey   105

Netheravon Dovecot   119
Netley Abbey   59
Nine Ladies Stone Circle   32

Nine Stones, The, Winterbourne
  Abbas 38
Norham Castle 90
North Elmham Cathedral and
  Earthworks 83
North Hinksey Conduit House 99
Northington: The Grange 58
North Leigh Roman Villa 99
Norwich: Cow Tower 84
Notgrove Long Barrow 44
Nunney Castle 105
Nympsfield Long Barrow 44

Odda's Chapel, Deerhurst 44
Offa's Dyke 45
Okehampton Castle 35
Old Bishop's Palace, Wolvesey 60
Old Blockhouse 69
Old Gorhambury House 63
Old Merchant's House and Row
  111 Houses, Great Yarmouth 83
Old Oswestry Hill Fort 102
Old Sarum 119
Old Soar Manor, Plaxtol 73
Old Wardour Castle 119
Orford Castle 110
Osborne House 67
Ospringe: Maison Dieu 73
Over Bridge 45

Paignton: Kirkham House 35
Pendennis Castle 25
Penrith Castle 30
Pevensey Castle 113
Peveril Castle 32
Pickering Castle 94
Piel Castle 30
Piercebridge Roman Bridge 94
Pike Hill Signal Tower 55
Piper Sike Turret 56
Planetrees Roman Wall 56
Plaxtol: Old Soar Manor 73
Plymouth: Royal Citadel 35
Poltross Burn Milecastle 56
Portchester Castle 59
Porth Hellick Down Burial Chamber 69
Portland Castle 38
Portsmouth: Garrison Church 59
Portsmouth: King James's and Landport
  Gates 59
Prior's Hall Barn, Widdington 42

Prudhoe Castle 90
Pyx Chamber, Westminster Abbey 51

Ranger's House 49
Ravenglass: Roman Bath House 30
Reculver Towers and Roman Fort 73
Restormel Castle 25
Richborough Castle 73
Richborough Roman Amphitheatre 73
Richmond Castle 95
Rievaulx Abbey 95
Roche Abbey 107
Rochester Castle 74
Rochester: Temple Manor 75
Rodmarton: Windmill Tump Long
  Barrow 45
Rotherwas Chapel 62
Row 111 Houses, Great Yarmouth 83
Royal Citadel, Plymouth 36
Royal Oak, Boscobel House and 101
Rufford Abbey 97
Rushton Triangular Lodge 86
Rycote Chapel 99

St Albans: Roman Wall 63
St Augustine's Abbey, Canterbury 74
St Augustine's Cross, Ebbsfleet 74
St Botolph's Priory, Colchester 42
St Breock Downs Monolith 26
St Briavel's Castle 45
St Buryan: Tregiffian Burial Chamber 26
St Catherine's Castle, Fowey 26
St Catherine's Chapel, Abbotsbury 38
St Catherine's Oratory 67
St Cleer: King Doniert's Stone 25
St Cleer: Trethevy Quoit 26
St James's Chapel, Lindsey 110
St John's Abbey Gate, Colchester 42
St John's Commandery, Swingfield 74
St Just: Ballowall Barrow 24
St Leonard's Tower, West Malling 74
St Mary's Church, Kempley 44
St Mary's Church, Studley Royal 96
St Mawes Castle 26
St Olave's Priory 84
St Paul's Monastery, Jarrow 114
St Peter's Church, Barton-upon-
  Humber 64
Salley Abbey 76
Sanctuary, The, Overton Hill,
  Avebury 119

Sandbach Crosses 22
Saxtead Green Post Mill 110
Scarborough Castle 95
Sewingshields Wall, Turrets and
    Milecastle 56
Shap Abbey 30
Sherborne Old Castle 38
Sibsey Trader Windmill 80
Silbury Hill 119
Silchester Roman City Wall 60
Sir Bevil Grenville's Monument 16
Skipsea Castle 64
Southampton: Medieval Wine Merchant's
    House 60
Spofforth Castle 95
Stanton Drew Stone Circles and Cove 16
Stanton Moor: Nine Ladies Stone Circle 32
Stanwick Iron Age Fortifications 95
Steeton Hall Gateway 96
Stokesay Castle 102
Stonehenge 120
Stoney Littleton Long Barrow 16
Stott Park Bobbin Mill 30
Studley Royal: St Mary's Church 96
Sutton Scarsdale Hall 32
Sutton Valence Castle 74
Swingfield: St John's Commandery 74

Tattershall College 80
Temple Church, Bristol 16
Temple Manor, Rochester 75
Thetford: Church of the Holy Sepulchre 84
Thetford Priory 84
Thetford Warren Lodge 84
Thornton Abbey 65
Tilbury Fort 42
Tintagel Castle 26
Titchfield Abbey 60
Totnes Castle 36
Tower of London 50
Tregiffian Burial Chamber, St Buryan 26
Trethevy Quoit, St Cleer 26
Tynemouth and Castle Priory 114

Uffington Castle, White Horse and Dragon
    Hill 99
Uley Long Barrow 45
Upnor Castle 75
Upper Plym Valley 36

Vindolanda Fort 56

Wall Roman Site (Letocetum) 108
Walltown Crags Wall and Turret 56
Walmer Castle 75
Waltham Abbey Gatehouse and Bridge 42
Warkworth Castle and Hermitage 91
Warton Old Rectory 76
Waverley Abbey 111
Wayland's Smithy 99
Weeting Castle 84
Wenlock Priory 103
West Kennet Avenue, Avebury 120
West Kennet Long Barrow 120
West Malling: St Leonard's Tower 74
Westminster Abbey Chapter House,
    Pyx Chamber and Abbey Museum 51
Westminster: Jewel Tower 48
Wetheral Priory Gatehouse 30
Weymouth: Jordan Hill Roman
    Temple 37
Whalley Abbey Gatehouse 76
Wharram Percy Church and Deserted
    Medieval Village 96
Wheeldale Roman Road 96
Whitby Abbey 96
White Horse, Uffington 99
White Ladies Priory 103
Widdington: Prior's Hall Barn 42
Willowford Bridge Abutment 56
Winchester Palace 51
Windmill Hill 120
Windmill Tump Long Barrow,
    Rodmarton 45
Winshields Wall and Milecastle 56
Winterbourne Abbas: The Nine
    Stones 38
Winterbourne Poor Lot Barrows 38
Witley Court 62
Wolvesey: Old Bishop's Palace 60
Woodhenge 120
Wrest Park House and Gardens 18
Wroxeter Roman City 103

Yarmouth Castle 67
Yarn Market, Dunster 104
York: Clifford's Tower 96

English Heritage
Subscription Categories 1990

TWELVE MONTH MEMBERSHIPS

Adult: £12.50.

Two Adults at the same address: £22.50.

Family: £25 for two parents and all children under 21 years. Each member receives an individual card.

Single Parent Family: £15 for one parent and all children under 21 years.

Senior Citizen: £9 for people aged 60 and over.

Two Senior Citizens at the same address: £16.00.

Young Person: £9 for people aged 16 and under 21 years.

Junior: £6 for the under 16's including membership of KEEP.

LIFE MEMBERSHIPS

Individual life: £250. This entitles a member to bring a guest at no extra charge.

Joint life: £325 for husband and wife, each receiving their own card. Up to four accompanying children under 16 years also admitted.

Senior Citizen life: £190 available to anyone 60 years and over. Entitles a member to bring a guest at no extra charge.

Joint Senior Citizen life: £240 for husband and wife aged 60 years and over each receiving their own card. Up to four accompanying children under 16 years also admitted.

Increase your contribution to England's Heritage without increasing your subscription

Your annual subscription helps us to protect England's most important historic heritage whilst giving you the freedom to visit any of our 350 properties absolutely free.

However, your subscription could go even further without costing you any extra. Paying by direct debit is easier and more convenient for you and helps us to reduce our administrative costs.

Just fill in the form on page 128 and return it to us.

It's so easy to increase your contribution to England's heritage – so why not change to paying by direct debit today.

Your bank account will not be debited until the month in which you membership is due for renewal.

English ⊞ Heritage

English ⊞ Heritage

Membership Application Form

Please first choose the membership category you prefer and then fill in the application form, preferably with the Direct Debiting Instruction overleaf as well, IN BLOCK CAPITALS. Please allow 28 days for delivery.

Send the completed form to: English Heritage Membership Department,
PO Box 1BB, London W1A 1BB.

✂ -

Tick the box for the membership category which suits you best:

TWELVE MONTH MEMBERSHIPS

☐ **Adult:** £12.50

☐ **Two Adults** at the same address: £22.50.

☐ **Family:** £25 for two parents and all children under 21 years. Each member receives an individual card.

☐ **Single Parent Family:** £15 for one parent and all children under 21 years.

☐ **Senior Citizen:** £9 for people aged 60 and over.

☐ **Two Senior Citizens:** at the same address: £16.

☐ **Young Person:** £9 for people aged 16 and under 21 years.

☐ **Junior:** £6 for the under 16's including membership of KEEP

LIFE MEMBERSHIPS

☐ **Individual life:** £280. This entitles a member to bring a guest at no extra charge.

☐ **Joint life:** £325 for husband and wife, each receiving their own card. Up to four accompanying children under 16 years also admitted.

☐ **Senior Citizen life:** £190 available to anyone 60 years and over. Entitles a member to bring a guest at no extra charge.

☐ **Joint Senior Citizen life:** £240 for husband and wife aged 60 years and over each receiving their own card. Up to four accompanying children under 16 years also admitted.

Source Code 0013

I/We wish to apply for the membership type I/we have ticked.

Please send me a membership pack.

†Mr/Mrs/Ms/Miss/Initials _____ Surname _____

Address _____

_____ Postcode _____

Date of Birth if under 21 _____
Additional members at the same address:

Partner: Mr/Mrs Initials _____ Surname _____

Juniors; Students:

Mr/Master/Miss Forename _____ Date of Birth _____

Mr/Master/Miss Forename _____ Date of Birth _____

Please attach a separate list if you wish to enrol more than two children.

The remittance for £ _____ is covered by the completed Direct Debit Instruction overleaf /is enclosed*/ may be debited to the credit card shown below.†

*Cheques should be made payable to ENGLISH HERITAGE.
†Direct Debit Instruction overleaf is applicable to ENGLISH HERITAGE.
†Please delete the sections not applicable.

Access/ Amex/
Barclaycard No. ☐☐☐☐☐☐☐☐☐☐☐☐☐☐☐☐

English ⊞ Heritage
Direct Debits

A direct debit enables English Heritage to receive your subscription directly from your bank. This saves us money, and it means that your membership card will be sent to you annually without the need for tiresome reminders.

This method also permits your subscription payments to continue without interruption, without the need for a fresh bank account if any mistake occurs.

mandate if the subscription rate increases. Prior to any subscription increase, we undertake to write to you well in advance of processing the debit.

You can cancel this authority at any time by instructing your bank and notifying us. Also, we have guaranteed to refund your

✂

INSTRUCTION TO YOUR BANK TO PAY DIRECT DEBITS

Please complete Parts 1 to 5 to instruct your bank to make payments directly from your account. Then return the form to:

English Heritage Membership Department, PO Box 1BB, London W1A 1BB

1. _____

TO THE MANAGER

PLEASE USE BLOCK CAPITALS

MEMBERSHIP NUMBER

☐☐☐☐☐☐☐☐☐☐

_____ BANK

_____ BRANCH

_____ POSTCODE _____

2. Name of account holder _____

3. Bank account number

☐☐☐☐☐☐☐☐

4. Bank sort code

☐☐ ☐☐ ☐☐

5. Your instructions to the bank and signature

* I/We instruct you to pay Direct Debits from my/our account at the request of English Heritage.
* The amounts are variable and may be debited on various dates.
* I/We understand that English Heritage may change the amounts and dates only after giving me/us prior notice.
* I/We will inform the bank in writing if I/We wish to cancel this instruction.
* I/We understand that if any Direct Debit is paid which breaks the terms of the instruction the bank will make a refund.

Signature(s) _____

Date _____

Banks may decline to accept instructions to charge Direct Debits to certain types of accounts other than current accounts.

Originator's Identification No. 940123